Hey Nata[...]
Your smile [...]
I met you somewhere else than
the E.R. I will be very happy
and glad to learn a little
about your travels around the
world.

WEEP,

TO A BELOVED

DESTINY

CHRIS B. MISSETT

Here a piece of my adventure
Enjoy!
Chris B mu

~ Chris B. Missett ~

The characters, events, and places in this book are nonfictions.

Also, by Chris B. Missett

A Window of Memories
As Far as I Miss You
Caged by Kidney Failure
Perfume and Bruises of a Life

WEEP, TO A
BELOVED DESTINY

DEDICATION

Gratitude and thankfulness

To Ms. Sandra M., Michelle C., Claudette C. and Mr. AJ., my heartfelt acknowledgment for your thoughtful and empathic actions, appreciation, and thankfulness are the honest praise that I replied to declare what your empathy and laugh for all you managed to me. To ignore your marvelous actions might win a life.

Particular thanks to Ms. Adriana H. for through, your sweet smiles and peals of mirth you let my soul laugh over true, wholehearted love.

And
to make up a good potential towards many of my philosophical friends on the "Facebook" I gape at their talents.

Thank you to all my readers! For any question, please contact me at c78mb@yahoo.com

PREFACE

Attracted by the blows of cutoff, the stalk of a change in the book of my way of life gradually shows up on a silent filter of my life story.

As clear droplets of reminiscences side by side have started a pool in which I reflect, pretty or shadowy images of what has existed or will ever prevail for the reminders of Madame Destiny.

The small "You" was the obstacle, concern of falling. The Will of God, and the "Me", the greater ego always defined or planned my long-term survival strategies. The daydreams and objectives were entirely in the vast gleams of yearning.

The dreams with sentimental afterglows held in the immensity of solitary loneliness. I journeyed in the land of fantasies and dreams of the time. In a languorous hush, I lived the inspirations of Madame Destiny.

Some stages of my way of life seemed like a bird, thinking to fly abroad, but a fowl without wings could not be a fowl, or as the man without aspirations could not be a man.

To build up dependence an understanding of being capable to make things by me, and for me was a school, the school was so long and difficult that "You" was sometimes panicking the "Me."

In favor's days, I was a product of the illusions of the night, a vision with an eager gleam stuck in the immensity of flawless solitude behind the recognitions.

Often, the "You" and "Me" traveled in the land of probabilities to mature, and develop a personal growth no matter how tough it was to create a story of my life, and I earned to learn upon it.

PROLOGUE

Youths who left their house are seen or described as bad, problematic, no good children or lonely…

With me, it was not like that; I wanted to change my life, to control my own destinies.

The inaudible voices of my dreams, my goals and the Will of God determined me.

The stronger character was some friendly teacher of "Me" and swaying me forward. Was it an absolute "Me" or a Will of God?

I enjoyed the challenges just like I enjoyed the loneliness.

So, I was giving up the warm, unconditional love of my family.

~ Chris B. Missett ~

FOUNDATION OF MYSTICISM

Feeling better that I had left my family; my communication with the higher self was most often, "Superb! I told you ... that you would get there!"

Longing to find my true destinies, like in romance, I was looking for my twin flame ... my real purpose and the purpose of my life was to process my strength, my confidence in myself and to follow all that my heart desired.

I was trying to accept myself as an alchemist, but I felt more humbled and grateful to God's will and endurance.

I was challenging alike as a juvenile. Looking at the diverse juveniles, I consistently felt that I had done nothing meaningful. Only my stronger ego in success can be built my myth.

CONTENTS

1 ~ PARENTAGE AND YOUTH

The father died four years ago; the mother was taking over the role of the father and the mother.

And even, being a single parent overwhelmed her and because of her age.

The grown-ups and the little ones, the working, the married or the eligible, all children were in as the appearing of helpmates.

The mother was a friend, a guide, and counselor. She was even a mentor and an educator for the youngest that I was.

When I was growing up, I had a dazzling baby face with bright eyes and a radiant smile with big dimples, and easy to spot among other children.

I had a passionate empathy that I had used for all human dealings. I was funny and am despite the weight of ages I was a dapper man.

I heard my thoughts in voiceover as I strolled home, "The twelve-year-old me imagined the thirteen-year-old me," my thoughts begun wistfully. "The thirteen-year-old me imagined the fourteen-year-old me. Now that I was reaching my fourteens, I kept looking and reality sunk in."

Growing up, I was wondering how I could be a tremendous support for my aging mother.

One spring evening, while my mother was preparing dinner, I joined her in the kitchen.

"Hi, mom, do you know how much I love your hands in produces while you cook?"

"Hi, your sisters are not here to help me today, can you help?"

"No mom, I enjoy watching you and admiring you ... in fact, do you remember what you tell me ... if I want to be a strong man, I have to learn to fight alone in my fights always have a smile so that nobody knows how much I could be crushed inside me.

She smiled at me, and squeezed me in her tender arms, "What do you have to tell me?"

"You know that you always add more to our family, Mom, if I left a distance between you and my brothers and sisters, I will never be far from you by my thoughts, will you still love me?"

"Tsit," she pushed me away, "My child, you are my crush because I love you since the first day, I opened my eyes on you."

I made a childish smile, "Mom, sometimes I heard incredible voices focusing on social change. I wanted to change and change my destiny."

In a warm and gentle voice, she replied, "My son let your human behavior be guided by a good instinct. Through good or bad decisions, be fair and able to control your own destiny. Convince the world that you want to live your visions and the dreams of your life."

I wrapped my arms around her waist. "Mom, I want to travel and discover the outside world!"

She looked at me. "I'm not sure… at fifteen!" she exclaimed, "You are still a child. There is a risk of depression, isolation, and even sometimes feelings of helplessness ... that is traveling with you? Do you want to walk away from your family?"

"Wow mom!" Why mothers can always read the mind of their children.

"Do you know how your decision will seriously affect your brothers and sisters and your friends?"

"I want to conquer me and prepare the best of tomorrow mom!"

She gently and tenderly holds me in her arms.

"Tsit…conquer you at fifteen? Why can't you conquer your brothers, sisters and me here? …Little baby."

"Oh mom, God will be my fate. There is no need to be afraid." I pleaded with her.

Then, mom and I both suddenly laughed.

"Oh, I see, God will be your fate!" Mom said smilingly.

Then, one sister popped up, briskly my conversation to be kept secret with mom ended.

"Thank you Delft, that was a lovely thing to know," Said Mom.

2 ~ IF I GO AWAY

I had a joyous family…with very great connection and great unconditional love for at decent home.

But, day from a day, I was living a conflict with tiptoeing into my destiny, the eyes of my family, friends and the views of society.

Will fantasies and illusions bring out the most perfect in me? If I was making a lousy decision, will I be a respectable individual?

Maybe it was a dream, maybe it was an illusion, but I'll accept the lessons of my life, and write a fairy tale of the purpose of my life with the ink of my emotions.

On the debris of the chapters of my past, I would dance with my unfulfilled dreams as companions. The desire to go away, and ended travel.

My decision will seriously affect my family, or my friends even some people. Some may not know it, but, a few will think about it all the time.

Let this journey of mine and freedom ring, if I failed, nobody gives a damn!

You and Me...

The higher-self and I bonded,
if I could know how far
my higher self could go.
No tenderness, no love where about,
a set of fantasies setting my life.

As long as higher-self and I
travel on a fertile journey,
where about I was, feeling
like in a country of asylum,
in the freedom of nothing.

Crazy dreams,
like a fantastic ballet of
the rhythm of illusions,
a tear in the corner of my eyes,
I become a distant vagabond.

My distress mixed with a laugh,
troubled by strong emotion,
my soul languishes and sighs,
"Be still."

3 ~ LIVING PARALLELS LIVES

The action of leaving my family and friends was a childish quick decision.

I wanted to look for adventure and see how the outside the world was better.

I was a teenager impressed by the movie character of 'James Bond 007.'

So, I prepared myself to live parallel lives, the life of a child of fifteen completely seduced by the ambition to change my destiny.

And the life of a teenager beguiled by a hero of the screen gently cradled by the fairy tales of human success in the outside world.

A big bump appeared in my throat. After dropping stormy tears, I wrote a few lines:

Mother I miss you, mom…

But my heart will always be yours.
Mom, we are bound to each other
For eternity,   I want you to understand,

Our hearts speak and they draw me to cry.
Even if I learn in the crowd without you,
The silence and the distance say you care.
My happiness and sadness are meaningless.

Mom, I'm numb by the cold,
I am fragile and alike a motherless child.
Tears in your eyes claimed
You will never leave me.

I want you to keep protecting me
in your extra gentle arms.
Mom! Let us meet again
In Heaven, would you?

The time I left the motherland to sulk around the world, I roughly turned fifteen-years-old.

~ Weep, to a Beloved Destiny ~

My mom did not want to see me leave, I was insane; I walked out the sole loving family I have had.

I had turned my back on my mother, my siblings, friends and I said "Farewell."

Like many fifteen-year-old boys, I was from a big family. I attended a large Jesuit college. I had good friends; they were great kids.

I wanted to travel the world.

It was early in mid-June; I had saved money through my small jobs in the neighborhood and my family had given me more the day of my departure.

Knowing that I was leaving the house, my mother and my sisters packed me. However, my mother did not want me to leave.

Why did my separation affect her so much that I was not her only son - did my mother love me much more than my siblings? I kept thinking about it.

My two sisters, Caroline and Sam had accompanied me to the bus station. When the bus of my future destination arrived, Caroline, Sam, and I exchanged emotional hugs.

They had not cried. Me neither, I had not cried for fear that they do not convince me to bring me back home.

Caroline advised me, "You'll never admit to having a lot of money," she added, "Always say you spent your last money."

I mumbled to them, "I'm leaving, be nice to Joe, no bad looks to Joe. Joe is now the only brother you have, take good care of my mother," I endured, "I'll stay in touch with you. I might stay in the neighbor country until I find a stable job. Maybe there, I'll have a happy life, wish me a stroke of good luck, I'll need it. Tell my mother that I'll do my best."

Sam warned me, "You have enough money, live a modest life and like a child, always say that you are waiting for your parents," her voice softened, "Nobody told you to leave the house, good luck with your decision. You must do your best and keep your religious values, anyone will accept you, and may God the Almighty bless you!"

Caroline glanced at me her eyes filled with tears, "Just do what your mother tells you."

"Sam is not my mother..."

Sam looked at me, "How many mothers do you have?"

"Just one,"

"Look here, you little runt, you have three mothers."

"Tsit, you are my sisters ... not my mothers!"

Caroline slower pulled on one of my ears, "Hey, do you want Sam and I call the police on you? And we will tell them that this little boy is running away from home?"

"Ouch, let go, it's not credible, do you both want to die, or else I kill myself, afterward, my mother will kill you both."

Caroline winked at Sam and they both started to laugh. It was funny because I too started to laugh watching them laugh at me. That was the last laugh with my well-beloved sisters.

I stepped on the bus hiding my emotional tears. When will I see my sisters again [...]?
I was straddling my destiny, or I was writing a new chapter in the story of my life.

4 ~ FAREWELL BELOVED HOMELAND

When I arrived in the town neighboring of the next state, I have to figure out a game plan to enter the next town neighboring the border of the country which was eventually my succeeding stride.

I made myself as invisible as possible. I hold on to the bits of advice that my two beloved sisters gave me, and maybe even to lie about my country of origin.

Making an associate was helpful, but, talking to the grownups could be harmful…that was plain out of a challenge. It was better to be alone than to be with someone who would cause, I break down.

~ Weep, to a Beloved Destiny ~

As I was a spoiled brat I liked to stay off the streets, and out of harms, I rented a hotel room to spend a few nights and days for a stay in the new town.

I just left home a day yet the next day; I invited myself to play a game of Soccer with local soccer players.

He was a teenager, very skillful and a good soccer player. I remembered we were sitting on the cold grass, as I recalled, I did not tell him my name that evening when he approached me.

"Hey, I would like someone to run with me," he said, his eyes looking elsewhere.

"I'm waiting for my parents, why do you want to run aren't you scared, running away from your parents is wrongdoing," I asked him in my way filled with sadness, "It's solitary, isn't it?"

That evening, when I went into my lodge lying on my bed I stammered:

> Here I am amidst the illusions,
> the focal spot of my current way of life.
>
> The tastes of my essence stare
> and laugh at the stars
> metamorphoses crowed my daydreams..

~ Chris B. Missett ~

A day after, it was in the same field, we were playing a soccer game. During a pause, the same stranger teen walked along the sideline, then came back and sat down next to me again.

"I have a lot of dreams ... A friend of mine is playing for a good team in Europe now ... so I want an adventurer. I have already crossed two countries."

"Let's go back a moment, you just have a bite for adventure?"

"I have great skills to play in different countries, maybe in a national league...to start somewhere again. I could not imagine throwing this life and starting a new life ... with a new name ... a new face ... in a new place ... a new beginning [...]"

"So what am I doing within it? I do not have good soccer skills," I told him

"What?" He replied.

Teenagers are humans and social animals. Defiant and silent, I began to enjoy with being close to another child on the run.

"Do you know that fleeing your home is illegal and an offense?

"I will not look back, I'm going forward for good and I know that I will not change my mind."

"And why do you want a travel companion? It's out of questions. I'm waiting for my parents."

He beckoned for me to join him and pointed the country across a very wide river. He looked at the wide river,

"See, that country over there is not-so-distant. But I can't cross that body of water alone."

There was silence.

I became silent and distrustful, yet I started to increase to pay attention to the words of a stranger boy. The strange was strange. Why would the crossing of the river be so important for his journey?

Focused on the disappointing gaps that emerged between the dreams of this seventeen years old adventurer, and the expectations for his life of a future soccer player, 'Friends are God's apology for relationships or parenthood.'

It prepared me not to answer questions from him, but I would give up some hints to my whereabouts. I was avoiding people who may have a lot of questions, and to resist the homesick and urge returning home.

Yet, I needed to make it as far away as possible I could.

I never hung around the same place for too long. My aging would be brutal day by day frightened by it.

With a boy, I just have known for a few hours. How could I trust him?

Our free passage from my homeland to the neighboring country was the first foot print of my voyage.

The crossing of the confluence insight required a study of the changes of the tides, a means of safe transport, a good captain to set the travel course and navigate the current towards the estuary, how to avoid the coast guards of two countries, the freshwater, and food for the excursion.

We rented a comfortable wooden skiff in the rest of the afternoon. With this boarding, we were ready to launch our trip.

We waited for the night to set down on the river, the land, and softened the currents of the water of the wide estuary. We stayed up to date on our schedule.

Although I was at the Jesuit Catholic School, I studied and I could and was a very serious student.

While the other children were reading cartoon books, such as "Tintin and Milou," I was reading "Battler Briton," a cartoon illustrating the heroic actions of a chef-pilot of the British Royal Squadron. I wanted to be a test pilot.

That night, I became a captain to ensure the safety and efficient operation of our travel of crossing. I recalled whispering, "Sam, look at me. I'm fifteen and I'm a captain. Leaving my family was my sail. I paddled; I paddled to my unnamed journey."

But, what will happen if slowly on, my traveling partner and I will face danger or questions, what do I know about a strange seventeen-year-old foreign soccer player, and again, our pact was so thin, like a slice of bacon.

I was sure that some European soccer teams would be lucky to have this prodigious youngster. He was a great soccer player in his youth.

God asked us to love one another, but God; drawing everything, how much love did I give you?

In the middle of the water became cold as ice, I began to suffer from an unknown solitude. I missed my family my sister Sam…my best friend.

Without a strength wanting to die, further, I did not want to go back home.

That night, I threw away the innocence of my childhood. I thought of my parents and I was not sure I did not like them because I was losing their unconditional love in my senseless adventure that looked like water on the sand.

The lights of the city went out, and the shores were dark, icy and dark. When the wooden skiff boat twinkled on the waters of the neighboring country, I pronounced my first farewell. Silent, I wept:

"Oh, Mother.

while the night crosses the river and the land,
the midst of darkness,
I sit down on the doorstep
of your garden of Eden of your love.

Sam my beloved sister,
it will be soon in the morning.
The sun will rise, will I hear
again the sound of your voice.

I left love for the insane illusions of a child.
Where am I going? Where is my pathway going?
My dear brother, all the faults
I committed against you, will you forgive me?

My heart will always love you.
My older sisters, I have no way to return your love.
I'm finished, I'm in pain. Such as the pain of
They nailed feet of Jesus Christ with a nail.

Mother, and my brothers and sisters,
fate has sent us in separate directions,

18

freedom ... and I choose the freedom
Offered to an intelligent child who will play

Mom, my heart will always love you.
With you, you were too proud of me.
Every day and night, in my prayers.
I will ask God to protect you, and also me.

We sailed and with elegance. We had crossed the big confluence. As soon as the wooden skiff hit the shore of the neighboring country, my traveling companion and I anchored our wooden skiff under a sloping tree branch over the water to protect us from anyone's sight.

The greed of adventure consumed my faithful traveling companion and me.

I felt like a prodigal child. I also felt like I was creating my retirement from my beloved family.

In the morning, we wanted to walk on the bank of the river but we feared the predators.

We opted to spend half the day in the skiff at the mercy of mosquitoes and scoping the surrounding. We spent the rest of the night telling each other the funniest stories of our lives to assure each other our friendship... moving speech about our dreams and fantasies.

It made our bond to seem rare because we didn't know each other where we came from.

Was he my God sent Angel? He must be a crazy Angel who desired the comfort of a friend like me [...]

We had been handed over to the officers of the customs police. Our eyebrows shot in panic. I told them we had come from Vienna, the capital. The city we wanted to go to.

We had no documents or papers to deal with the law enforcement officers but; they believed us.

Yet, when a customs officer searched our backpacks, he discovered that my traveling companion had a Soccer Ball in his backpack.

I wondered why he was carrying a Soccer Ball in his gear

It was at the satisfaction for customs officers to know that we knew how to play football or maybe we would be good future players.

This was how a Soccer Ball provided us fertile ground with the officers. We discussed football, they displayed their knowledge of certain famous players, the great matches and some memorable past World Cups.

A friendship has begun to build between them and us. We were well fed and later sent to the immigration authorities without any harms.

The Immigration guards believed our story as we maintained our false identities throughout the process.

In the meantime, I was nicknamed *Walking Encyclopedia* because I could speak a few words of their language and my companion was nicknamed *Soccer Ball* from his soccer ball.

It was fun, but at the time we could not find it really fun.

It took us three days to know where we were coming from and where we were going. It was a long wait and awful suspense without purpose.

With the help of God, they deported us to the city of Salzburg, Austria.

I tried my luck and had a free ride. We appreciated the deception that led us to take another step in our path.

We never remember the day, this moment, but we made it the best memory of our trip...

"Hey you, *Walking Encyclopedia*, it's your turn to tell me something," asked. *Mr. Soccer Ball.*

"About, what? There is not much to tell you, dear mister!"

"Still, you have not shown where your parents were, and why they were waiting for you?"

"I am an adventurer…if I fail. it was forever," I added, "The Psalm 28 will help me in my journey."

"Holy, cow! Then, you're just running away like me…"

"Yes, and I'm going somewhere or my destiny leads me, leave it or take it. Using a prank sprouted a great victory for us. We are still alive, so God is with us. For the better or the worse, it's time for us to control our own destiny." I continued, *"Soccer Ball-"* do not explain yourself to anyone, the person who doesn't like you will not want to believe you."

"No worries."

"What?"

"Well--"

"Oh, my God, Kiddo, wait, I do not even know your name!" he said.

I laugh. It does not matter, "Just call me Delft …"

Soccer Ball stared at me absently and winced.

"What?"

"Now, remember, I never explain myself to anyone … again, take it or leave it, sir …" I said.

"Delft, can you tell me about your family?"

"I do not have any …"

"Liar, well, you're just a child, are you suppose to come from a family or somewhere?

I laughed, then silent for a few seconds. I sighed. Tears ran down my cheeks."Well, *Soccer Ball,* you know what, the scariest thing is not knowing if I was missed by my family and friends. But, I allowed a distance to them. I was never far away from them by my thoughts."

"Why?"

"Because, fleeing from home does not mean that I was a delinquent, a bad or dangerous child. At home, they have always given me a top priority. I was respected and loved. I was the idol of my family. Now, sincerely, would you tell me your name in return? "

"Carl ... my name is Carl. And I greet the God in you *Encyclopedia,* and giving you my goodwill," he said.

"Wow, it sounds wonderful in my heart, Carl, you are just on the adventure like me, now, this is my humor," I declare.

"Silly kiddo!" he laughed, "Kiddo, trusting your own intuition will make you feel lonely."

"Kiddo!" I echoed him, "Carl if you rely on someone else, he'll let you down."

"But you have not let me down still."

"Well, Carl, you do not know me that long enough."

"Silly kid, whatever, now, tell me about yourself."

"Like that?"

"I do not know, a joke, a fact about this world, something as settling here and there. The adventure may kill you, for example, your last girlfriend, or finding one girlfriend."

I looked at him for a moment "Oh, my God, I never had one," *now he became a CIA, KGB officer or what?* I whispered.

"What?"

"I never had a girlfriend!"

"Ah, are you a saint or a virgin?" He laughed aloud, "So, you have no emotional attachment of heart... you're in a good position for a runaway."

"Hey, I'm fourteen and a half. I was an altar lad in my Creed. I am going to climb the Himalaya…Go to Sweden the country stock of beautiful blonde girls, you know --"

"Aha, you go! It's your Journey, is your fate-" He replied.

"Fate of a boy who did not hesitate to flee from his parents and his country to wander like a wreck driven by the waves of dreams and ambitions of a teenager?" I rolled my eyes to him.

"Listen, kiddo, you can make a lousy decision, but you're a valuable person."

"Tsit,"

There, we both laughed.

I thought he'd never get over calling me 'kiddo' or '*Walking Encyclopedia.*'

"Okay, *Soccer Ball,* I'm drained and starving. Let's go rent a cheap room at some cheap Hostel."

"Silly," he paused. "Do you have some money?" He asked.

"Ha-ha, you poor delinquent, how did you crossed three countries, robbing dead people? I have my last 60 Deutsch Mark." I babied him.

"Kiddo, where did you pick up the money?"

He was treating me like a kid anew because he is just three years older. "I found it!" I growled.

"But Delft, we don't have passports or identity papers?"

"Come on…we have immigration's process papers."

"They are acceptable. We will go tomorrow to our Consulate for expedited provisional passports and identification documents." I suggested.

Carl looked at me, shook his head side to side, "Where had you learned all those tricks?"

I looked at the blue sky, "When you were playing soccer. Aha!"

"Let's go," Carl urged, walking ahead of me.

We walked to the train station. We read the info of one international hostel. After ten minutes of walk whereabouts, we arrived at the YOHO international hostel.

The hostel staffs were friendly. Some speak German, Polish, other French, English, Russian and native Austrian, if I forgot any. An incredible mixture of international languages, I felt like in a little immersion of languages learning.

"Delft, I will cover your three nights…I owe you thanks."

"Thanks for what?" I asked.

"For your pranks, that led us here."

I was astonished to see such appreciation. "Wait…I don't even know where you are from?" I said with twinkles in my eyes.

"You mean my parents? Kiddo, remember, we're just friends."

"Oh, good explanation," I chuckled.

"The mother was a Belgian, the father a Slovenian. No matter, "he softens his voice, "Now, it's all true!"

I never want to lose his friendliness, "And I am a child of the American army left behind. My father was killed in Vietnam. I'm sorry; there is nothing more to say!"

Carl booked three nights, a bunk bed with an individual locker in a mixed male and female dorm. He took the bed from the top.

I was not sure that such a world exists. I was wondering what to think when I look at this, years later.

The hostel was a perfect place to meet other young travelers and backpackers from around the world. It was a good place to get more information to plan the next trip and guess a city to call a new city of origin.

We were very excited. We found a satisfactory, safe and ideal place to meet other travelers. The next morning, we went to introduce ourselves to the consular offices of our respective countries in order to legalize ourselves.

The rest of the day, I pushed aside my hero James Bond 007. I became much inspired by the efforts a few heroes young children orphans survival of World War I and II.

Like them, with my travel companion, we decided to look for a possible grape harvesting job with other backpackers.

It was a safer and smarter way to make a little more money to travel and discover as many countries in Europe.

Later in the evening, I bought Carl a dinner in a good restaurant.

The following day at the Consulate, we were identified as teenage runaways who lacked identifications. The process of issuance of a temporary passport or a travel document took us almost one month.

While waiting for the process, we opted to work grape harvest at a big vineyard working part-time and living in the farm's compound trying to earn and save enough money to continue our adventure.

When we were offered the job, we moved from YOHO to Ferienhof the whereabouts the sunny Hof Bei hill. It was a good turnout. It was not too crowed. We liked the job and enjoyed a serene life.

"I will pay you well if you like farming and do good work!" The farmer said.

We worked for one month and a half. Our labels of *Soccer ball* and *Walking Encyclopedia* became a source of momentary amusing anecdotes.

Carl started dating a girl who worked with us. She was very friendly and pretty.

Carl liked him. She was hot but not very elegant. She told us that she came from Vienna, Austria.

A few weeks later, Carl and the girl disappeared from the farm.

It hit me. I did not need this bad surprise at this point. I could not ask anyone about Carl. It was very difficult for me. My heart started to hurt.

"Tsit - bloody puberty, what was wrong with our trip, Carl? Oh, false hope unsuccessful. I did not understand," then I smiled, "I did not want to understand. What nonsense. Carl, where are you? I need you, but I do not want you and I do not want to find you."

It filled me with pain and fear of being alone. Till now, I kept wondering, *"Who helped whom ...Carl or I?"*

I persisted in a few words, *"Bye Carl, I think you're safe where you are. Having met you will always be a part of my life."* A vivid emotion overwhelmed me; intense memories reminded me of Carl during the crossing of the river. Well, the time seemed like a river. I could not touch the same water twice, because the flow that passed will never pass again.

I wondered in which city in Austria Carl was. May-be I'll ask him how he is doing in the city. I wanted Carl to succeed.

At my side, I was very upset and guilty of leaving my family and home for a crazy dream.

Little by little, the journey seemed like a struggle for survival. Well, some experiences of my getaway had to been living instead of being told. I closed my eyes and recited a small prayer.

I remembered that some people enter our lives and leave, some stay for a moment and leave a mark on our hearts. And we will never be the same.

I needed freedom and luck to change my social life. I thought only a trip outside of my family, friends and home country could allow me to control my destiny.

Lonesome adventurer…

When the sun will rise in the sky,
Young adventurer, start your walk again.
Learn new skills.
New plans and new knowledge
of your endless journey.
Do everything with distinction.

I was emotionally in need of my mother and siblings. But, when I closed my eyes, I felt so lonely but, there was no next time, I had just started my trip!

5 ~ TRAVEL TO THE LAND OF FANTASIES

I remembered my mother always told me, 'If you want to be strong, learn to fight alone. Smile and no one will see how you are broken inside.'

I was feeling good. When people move away from me, they never tied their destiny to mine. It does not mean they are bad people. It can mean the part in my story has made. I was going where led my road...

I knew the path I took would long-drawn-out. A traveling companion can get in and out of my trip because of the choice of my risk and my ambitions.

Only God can replace them as fast as they walk on me. I will not forget them. I have to learn to appreciate them. They are my strangers with keepsakes.

Many teenagers and European backpackers travel a lot in Europe. The residents of E.U., countries (European Common Market) do not need a visa to visit neighboring countries.

The Youth hostels are a cheap budget to take advantage of. Some sometimes even offer light meals.

Some of my readers may think meeting European teenagers and locals were difficult because of the barrier of language or race. But, always being nice, open, and saying "hello" and "yes" in a different language could entice that bit of pride that comes from afraid of making local friends and good memories.

I was lucky enough to cross a border from the list of countries I had to cross.

Decent transport across a border, while other passengers were sleeping, it will also depend on not getting caught and thrown in jail.

My first joke will it will use My first joke an example. "It does not matter if it does not work; I can find many more–I have to be positive - I have to become more familiar with the geography of Europe and the customs controls. I will never give up my dreams! "

~ Weep, to a Beloved Destiny ~

Solitude…

Solitude my companion!
In my reveries you follow me
like my shadow.

With my solitude,
your echoes in my ears
They weigh down my heart.

My solitude! Untainted memories
and hot distress overflow my eyes,
quietly, my tears streamed…

6 ~ A MIRACLE

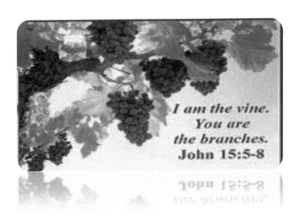

I am the vine. You are the branches. John 15:5-8

After two weeks of work on the farm. One day, I received a call from the consulate through the farmer to retrieve my traveler's document.

A heavy feeling of comfort enveloped me: "Heavenly Father, are you really there? It's a miracle ... What a miracle!" I sighed and felt stronger than ever.

I quickly knelt at the foot of a plant of the vine. I looked at the Firmaments: "Heavenly Father, your love now surrounds me. Oh Eternal, how would you show me to distill a better way to realize my dream in such a complex journey?"

A gentle voice surprised me: "Who are you?"

"Uh, me ... I'm just a teenager motivated by a childish dream."

"What is your dream?" The voice said.

I looked around to see who was talking to me, and then shyly, "I left my family to look for my destiny."

"And what is your destiny?" The voice asked.

"What do I know about my fate?" I replied, "I'm only traveling with the Will of God...I just started my journey."

"Well, many teens have started their destiny but many things have attracted their attention and they have abandoned their goals or they have stopped." The voice said.

"Oh, good!"

"Some fairy tales of successful young people gives you confidence?" The Voice asked again.

"Oh, this is a plant of vine that talks, a genie or an Angel of God?" I asked the voice. "Do you want to come with me and, to inspire me along my journey?"

"I am a glimmer of hope that touches you, it's time to learn your emotions, your decisions and prove to the world what you can do." the voice said.

"Huh?"

"Everyone can dream, but few of them can realize their daydreams, it is difficult to choose the unknown." the voice said.

"Listen, mister, there are many people who give up their dreams, and they are not bad people."

"Who are you?" the voice asked.

"I'm just a glimmer of hope that touches you, it's time to learn your emotions, your decisions and prove to the world what you can do." The voice stated.

"Huh?"

"Everyone can dream, but few of them can realize their dream, but it is difficult to choose the unknown." The voice implied.

"Listen—mister, there are many people who to give up their dreams, and they are not bad people."

"Though you struggle and suffer, you will never succeed at anything, if you do not merge with your dreams." and the voice added, "Do you like grapes?"

"Though you struggle and suffer, you will never succeed at anything, if you do not merge with your dreams." and the voice added, "Do you like grapes?"

"Yes, I do!"

"I am the Vine; you are the branches. If you remain in me and I in you, you will bear much fruit; apart from me, you can do nothing." John 15:5, --

Well, the juice of my grapes will flow in you like a river of strength and flexibility, warmth, enthusiasm, and creativity, patience, thoughtfulness, practicality, hard work, the Alchemist, persistence, strength, determined-nation, the softness, reserved and, still but also fearfulness!" The Voice stated.

"I will buy Inter-Rail used by travelers' under twenty-six years of age, a Global-Pass helps to travel in up to thirty countries to meet new peoples, new languages, and new cultures. I want to enjoy the breathtaking sceneries and every moment of my Journey. The trains are modern and dependable. They are the second form to travel in Europe after the airlines. Sometimes they can offer long hours of security checks at the borders."

"Now you have proper the identification you're capable of surviving to aim for more and to propel yourself to create your personal legend, or, to capitulate you have a home to go back to." The voice said.

Then, I stood up. I bowed my head, feelings of emptiness wrapped me. I was an introverted teen kind shy. How could I make new friends?

After Carl disappeared from me, I wanted to distance myself from everyone to hide my deep sense of being frozen by my fear. I did not want to attract attention or to blend in with other people.

I differed from others, however, very benevolent and easy to approach. Some people, I was curious and excited to meet me and to know me. Sometimes I only put a candid or calm smile on my face to start a converse with other workers.

A good few had the taste of laughing out loud at my pranks and seemed very willing to befriend to me.

Whatever country I wanted to go to, I tried a little to deepen my cultural and linguistic knowledge and to overcome my fear of the unknown.

The work on the farm was great. But the grape gathering was not my ideal job for my long life.

I had to work as a fact to earn extra money. I was not a disposable teenager.

My family members gave me money, and they promised to send me more when I needed some to make sure I would not end up a homeless teenager.

Would my trip complete my destiny? Only a morose solitude answered the echo of the song of my ambitions.

I was going where my glittering pathway was leading me...

7 ~ A POSITIVE WORLD TRAVEL

I was born in a US military barracks in Ansbach, in the south of West Germany. My father was an American G.I. killed in Vietnam four years after my birth.

It was during the Cold War after the Second World War. I was only fifteen, three socialist countries to go through (Austria, Czechoslovakia and the Republic Democratic of eastern Germany.)

In fact, each border had its own complications.

The traffic of the East Germany authorities was slow and difficult. The Locomotives and the crew of leach train were alternated at each entry or exit boundary.

The East German Transport Police (TRAPO) conducted the inspections at each post.

Sometimes an entry and exit visa required. The crossing of East Germany required me to live in the same city in Denmark with the young Danish couple, my new friends.

We laughed and chuckled when I told them about my plan to "hide under a seat or a banquette" at every checkpoint within the borders of East Germany.

I was not in a scarcity of money and not afraid of a fine, not worried about the ticket controller agents either. I had all my tickets.

But, bothered about the Russian army, therefore that I invented a scenario necessary to hide under a seat or a banquette of the train.

As an adventurer, I did not have big dreams for the future. My essence was the guide of my real life.

All I had was to keep positive values, and my inspiration for social change focused on my destiny.

After two more weeks of work, I saved a little more money, I studied my way. I wanted so much to make new friends for travel.

Well, like one says, "Never say never again." One day, a young Danish couple befriended me while it was time for them and me to leave Austria for the Kingdom of Denmark their homeland.

> *"Yesterday Carl and I were crossing the Danube,"*
> *"Yesterday Carl and I were in Salzburg, Austria,"*
> *"Tomorrow I will walk around Vienna, Austria,"*
> *"Tomorrow perhaps I will be crossing Czechoslovakia,"*
> *"Tomorrow perhaps I will be in East Germany,"*
> *"Tomorrow perhaps I will be back in West Germany,"*
> *"Tomorrow maybe I will be in the Kingdom of Denmark,"*

I was not happy to be an adventurer, but, I had the ambitious route planned by my higher-self, and the Will of God, and also my essence like a guide. For good or bad I had to control my own destiny.

My friends from Denmark and I went to Salzburg to get a lovely informative Lake Region small-group day-trip from Salzburg to Vienna with some of the exciting ideas regarding how to spend our weekend in Vienna.

This was our first time in Vienna. It was a great trip with great directions, an eye-opening experience, with a very knowledgeable guide.

We had two days to spend and explore the beautiful city of Vienna.

We visited Vienna and its various landmarks including quick visits to a few museums and Churches.

It was an excellent introduction to de Vienna.

Vienna was also known by many as one of the most romantic cities. It was the perfect destination for the young Danish couple, my friends.

Vienna was hypnotizing, captivating, known as the home of Opera, and Beethoven. Each passer-by creates memories of theirs.

We spent two nights at the Brigittenau Youth Palace Hostel, which has a garden and a shared lounge.

The facilities at this hostel included a restaurant, a 24-hour front desk and a large showcase for luggage storage.

After two nights at Brigittenau youth hostel, we booked three more extra nights, at Wombats City Hostel in Naschmarkt.

It was a perfect place to stay with its proximity to all major sightseeing sites. Wombats the hostel was located close to trains and public transport.

It was also ideal for anyone who wanted to explore Vienna by day or at night.

The place was wonderful because we could meet different people visiting Vienna for the first time. They offered us free maps, accommodation, and other destinations in Europe, just like travelers caring for travelers.

I was in Vienna, Austria. I started saying;

> *"Days ago I was in Salzburg, Austria,"*
> *"One week I was in Vienna, Austria,"*
> *"A few days ago I stayed in Prague, Czechoslovakia,"*
> *"Two days I toured in Dresden, Germany,"*
> *"Four days ago I was in Berlin, Germany,"*
> *"Day ago I was in Rostock, Germany,"*
> *"For days I will be in Odense, Denmark,"*

I had an ambitious route planned in the next few days. I'll have time to discover so many places, many people, different languages and cultures.

Even though I was adventurous, I was not a happy adventurer. Fear was an interesting companion because it was usually about the unknown or about situations that could happen without it happening to me.

~ Weep, to a Beloved Destiny ~

My dear friend fear was also a great motivation to overcome my challenges and obstacles. My fear as a shadow was also a sign of my willingness to take risks, change and grow.

8 ~ IT WAS TIME TO TRAVEL ON

I defined the pursuit of my dreams as a long and often difficult process of my change and my development; Traveling from one place to another was a positive inspired action me to fulfill some of my goals.

Hours ago, we were on the train going to Denmark. Denmark was a neighboring country in northern Germany.

Many Danes spoke and understood one or more foreign languages.

In the absence of Danish, they could use Basic English or German.

It was during the Cold War, travelers to and from Austria, Czechoslovakia, and Denmark could also transit through East Germany.

The West Germans (FRG) could also cross the border of East Germany (GDR).

During the crossing of Czechoslovakia and East Germany, I had to travel in the same the compartment of a train with the young Danish couple - my new friends.

We had a good laugh explaining to them my plan to "hide under the seat or the bench of the transport train" at every checkpoint in the East Germany republic.

Not concerned about ticket agents. I had all my tickets - I was rather afraid of the Russian army because of my young age to travel without parents or guardian.

I wanted to travel with less risk of being arrested. If they caught me, they could send me to prison.

This is how I had to create a scenario. And, the simplest way to play hide and seek with the Russian army TRAPO (The police of transport), FRG could also cross the border of East Germany (GDR).

Today my trip will be as smooth as it would be.
"Okay, Delft, just relaxes," The Danes said.
"I'm relaxed," I insisted.

Okay, that's a lie. It petrified me teen traveling with US traveler's document through Czechoslovakia, and GDR (East Germany)!

"There is no need to be nervous." The Danes said soothingly.

"No worries," I said. "How did I get myself into this trouble? I tried to calm myself by focusing on the sceneries of the road to travel. The silence was my source of great strengths," I whispered.

Mum!
Happy adventurer or vagabond,
deep within me lives a divine creature.

Mum!
Despite being so far away   from you, your
heart and mine are talking to each other.

Mum!
I see you in all things,
ready to protect me and have faith in me.

Mum!
Loneliness and distress envelop me.
I am like a child without a mother.

Mum!
It was not fair to leave.
It is now that I must go on my way.

Mum!
Should my accursed fear disappear?
My journey sparkles.

Mum!
Only intuition and endurance
will tell my unfortunate destiny.

While East Germany Transport Police (TRAPO) officers scanned the passengers looking at their faces.

I did not have to spend time under siege during the crossing of East Germany.

It passed, only one of them glanced at my travel documents, he frowned;

"No entry visa? What are you doing here?"

Ignoring a hint of nervousness, "Me, sir, I only want to visit the GDR, I said," it's an exquisite country!"

The officer seemed satisfied. He scrutinized my papers he found out that my travel document issued in Austria.

"Salzburg, Austria," he winced a smile. Then, he narrowed his eyes at me, "What were you doing there?"

I avoided eye contact, "Ouch. To be honest Mr. officer, I was visiting a friend, and I lost my passport sir."

"Sure," he smiles at me, "You must have been so scared?"

I dropped my head. How did he perceive that was I panicked? I told no one about my worry;

"No sir, I solely missed my parent."

"You act?" the TRAPO said.

The Transport Police officer was no longer looking at my travel document. If he would have leafed through, he would have found Czechoslovakia's stamps.

The agent TRAPO seemed very nice to me. I wondered if he had delinquent children as I was.

He looked at me and smiled again, "You Americans, adults or teenagers, you are all the Same. You aren't under arrest. There is no need to be scared. Enjoy your trip. Sicher sein, be prudent!"

I wondered if his words were so complimentary. I smiled back at him and offered him a chocolate bar from Austria. "Danke," I thanked him.

He shook his head, "Wenig zugvogel, little migrant bird," He winked at me and walked away hiding his laughter.

It was nearing three hours the train blew the whistle. It was a perfect immense relief. All passengers could breathe now.

It was fun. It was like a movie. A few hours later, I was back in West Germany hundreds of kilometers away from East Germany traveling to Denmark.

I cemented a memory in my heart for a long time. I always wanted to do it again.

I did not want to go back home. I was eager to learn more about different cultures, of Denmark.

Discover joy, laughter and to blend in Danish society—such was the will fate of a lonely teenager adventurer.

9 ~ ROSTOCK TO GESDER

Rostock was the largest city and port in North-East Germany where the War now River flows into the Baltic Sea.

They devastated the city of Rostock in WWII. I wish I was not on the run; I would freely visit the twenty-two gates and the beautiful beach of Rostock.

I just wanted to go out of East Germany as fast as I could. From the train station, the young Danish couple and I took the bus to the harbor.

At the ferry's terminals, I had my first encounter with seagulls bearing down with speed and accuracy to steal people's food.

Sailing from Rostock to Gesdser with Scand lines; I had booked in advance my sailing tickets as the young Danish couple my new friends advised me.

During the crossing, above the sea, the almighty albatrosses with their wings at a full stretch like kites were flying in every direction to attain the clouds.

Time to time I peered in the blue waters of the Baltic Ocean wondering, how many sailors, planes, ships even tanks drowned lying at the abyss of this ocean.

Was I sailing? The ferry ride was quick and punctual.

Three hours, from Rostock, Germany, we arrived at the port of Gesdser, the southernmost point of Denmark.

Gesdser was the important port city of the Baltic Sea and the first place where Germany troops landed during the occupation of the Kingdom of Denmark in the 1940s.

My friends and I were exhausted. We looked for a bed-and-breakfast.

I felt partly happy and partly torn by remorse. I allowed a great distance with my family and my friends, but I was never far from them beyond my thoughts

~ Chris B. Missett ~

I was a crazy teenager. My sister Sam, my best friend, missed me.

Tomorrow I had to call her and we would laugh well, I was alive - I became Viking.

Not my mother. She would scream or melt in the cry. Mothers have always been very good at it.

Languorous loneliness weighed down emotionally. Spiritually and physically up on me, was I step into my destiny or just re-writing the yesterday's story of my life?

Madame Destiny!

Maybe it's a crazy dream.
Maybe it's a crazy illusion.
Docile, I accept the lessons of a lifetime.

The chapters of mon voyage will be written
with the ink of my emotions.
I will dance on the ruins of my past.

I will recreate my adventure with sighs
in my eyes at every twinkling sun.
I had an amazing life so far.

~ Weep, to a Beloved Destiny ~

I will keep in my heart,
the reminiscences of the places I have been,
and the people I have met.

10 ~ I AM WELL AND ALIVE!

I went on the phone to call home, able to keep out the confusion in my voice. I listened to the phone ring twice. Then there was someone at the end of the line. I had Kelly.

"Hello - it's Kelly."
"Hello Kelly, did I take you in the middle of something?" I asked in a hidden voice.
"No!"
"Uh ... I'd like to talk to Sam."
"I give you Sam."
"Hello, this is Sam."
"Hi Sam, uh - how are you doing?" It's a little trick.

Silence, the phone cried, relieved by the tone of my voice.

"Oh, my God!" Sam exclaimed to Kelly and Mom: "It's Delft — Delft, where are you? How are you?" Sam sobbed, and she pressed the button of the speaker, "Mom, Kelly, here is our Delft!"

"Sam, our Delft --?" My mother and Kelly asked hesitantly in altered voices.

"Sam and Kelly please no yelling and swearing," It was Mom's voice warning.

"Mom, Delft is alive somewhere." Sam happily said.

"Kind of… I'm in Denmark and calling you from Denmark." I said.

"How did you get up there?" Sam, Kelly, and mom said in a close voice.

"By the trains, I crossed Austria, Czechoslovakia, East Germany, and then northern West Germany." I said.

Again silence.

"Wow, Little Runt, and you are well, no broken bones?" Sam asked.

"Yeah Sam, and I'm talking to you."

"Delft, you really did that alone?" Kelly asked.

"Kelly, Mon Voyage was fun, educational, exciting but scary. As soon as I arrived in Denmark, I forgot all the scariest part of the trip was passing in and out East Germany. You do what is fair and right to all living things there is nothing to be afraid of. For God gently commands the Angels over you and His Angels have many faces. At first, with the rented wooden skiff, I crossed the Danube River during the night with a runaway teen. We were both thrown in jail for two days after."

"Ha, Delft maybe you are calling us from jail," Sam said.

Kelly hushed Sam. "Sam, let him continue!"

"They deported us to Salzburg, Austria. At Salzburg, I went to the U.S. Consulate and applied for a passport. While waiting for new identification, I worked with other teens and travelers in a farm nearby Salzburg to gather grapes. My first traveling companion left me but I made new friends. Salzburg is the birthplace of Wolfgang Amadeus Mozart, and the Mozart Kugeln a famous dark chocolate cake. When it was time to move on, I went to Vienna, a spotless city with its many attractions. I visited the Haus Der Musik [with its history of prodigy composers like Beethoven, Hayden, Leopold Mozart my favorites,] and the State Opera House. Some attractions like the magnificent Schönbrunn Palace [the most visited, the residence to various Habsburg rulers,] and the Church of Jesuits. I ate a few delicious pastries in Vienna."

"Silly, Little Runt, why you didn't send me some," Sam grumbled.

"No worries Sam, I ate enough for both of us."

"Ha!" Mom and Kelly laughed at Sam.

I rode the train to Czechoslovakia. I liked Prague. The main attraction was the Old Town of Prague, the Jewish Center and Prague Castle. I blazed a trail to East Germany. I was terrified."

"It was just like when I visited Ireland. Catholics and Protestants fighting in the streets!" said Kelly, and she continued, "Delft! Sam was crying all the time for you. She missed you a lot."

"Kelly, don't we all do!" Sam grumbled.

"What else Delft..?" Kelly tried to laugh over the emotional sadness.

"Kelly! Crossing East Germany borders I was to enjoy going through severe watchful eyes. Soviets and East Germans were harassing travelers to weed out potential defectors. It carried the inspections of trains at the stations out by transport police using sniffer dogs to uncover stowaways, and to processed visas at the borders' stations."

There was again a silence at the other end of the line.

"Delft, can you imagine how worried and distressed your mother was," Sam asked.

"Sam — that's why mothers are irreplaceable; they can give life or exchange their life as best and precious gift to their children."

"I would like to see Delft's face if the Transport Police sic a police's dog on him!" exclaimed Kelly.

"Kelly, please, would you leave Delft alone! He is our youngest brother." Sam pleaded.

"Yea, but he walked out on us!" Kelly whispered.

"I wanted as soon as to go out of East Germany when we arrived at Rostock - Rostock was a pleasant surprise.   I discovered a delightful town with the Gothic German's architecture and a wide sandy beach.

As soon as I saw ferries from Denmark, I forgot all about the scariest part of my Journey. My heart was racing for Denmark. I tried to tell myself it was the scenery, but I knew it was part of my bucket list. The thought of mon voyage was thrilling. Traveling on trains was a glorious experience. Good people I met seemed they were God sent from heaven to me - Angels have many faces."

"Hey, wait a minute, Delft, God sent Angels over some little runt walking away from their well-beloved family? Aren't you fearful of traveling all alone?" Sam asked.

"Sam, I love you, I miss you, but I want to confront my fate with confidence, and control my destiny."

"Did you found it?"

"Not yet – but,"

The telephone sighed, it was mom.

"You see Sam, anxiety brings uncertain futures. What we have to do is not to judge and impede your sibling Delft. We have to make a way that he can head in a better direction." Mom said.

The telephone began weeping at the other end of the line.

"Sam, Kelly, mother, I was very excited to hear from you. I miss my sibling, Joseph. I love you all. I am cold. Please, can you hang up?" I pleaded wiping my tears while hiding my sobs.

"No, you hang up," Sam begged. "Little Runt, it was scary. I miss you, buddy."

A stream of tears rolled on my cheeks. I sobbed like a little child, "I miss you all," I mumbled and hung up.

By the time my first phone call to my family ended. I was in a torrent of tears. I felt once again the loneliness of a child on the adventure […]

I did not understand what the future held for me, always hoped that there were a lot more adventures left to do;

> *I was finally somewhere,*
> *as in a country of asylum.*
> *Without a trap, without a prison,*
> *in graceful freedom.*

> *Crazy dreams in a fantastic ballet*
> *past moments.*
> *Crazy dreams in a fantastic ballet*
> *present moments.*

~ Chris B. Missett ~

A tear at the corner of the eye
mingles with the laughter
of strong emotion, nothing
but the future was a risk.

11~ THIS JOURNEY OF MINE

The Danes enjoyed socializing with people whom they had grown up.

My friends, Gustav and Silije had welcomed me as a guest. We created our rare and valuable link from Austria. Most people around us would not understand or not like it.

The childhood friends of Gustav and Silije no longer lived near them. Maybe my adaptation facilitated by our friendship. Each of us desired the comfort of a friend.

The Danes particularly liked socializing with peole whom they had grown up.

My friends, Gustav and Silije had welcomed me as a guest. Our rare and valuable link was created from Austria. It seemed that the majority of people around us would not understand or not like it.

The childhood friends of Gustav and Silije no longer lived near them. Maybe my adaptation has been facilitated by our friendship. Each of us desired the comfort of a friend.

Silije had the gentle nature; she had blond hair, a radiant face with beautiful blue eyes and a soft voice. She was not very tall - rather petite.

It was always cold in Denmark even during the summer. Danish's summers have often been marked by rains and frost.

Gustav and Silije seemed more interested in learning French, German and English than Danish.

They had an ambitious itinerary planned in the coming years. If you had a lot of time, maybe you would know them!

A week later, Gustav and Silije offered me a memorable tour of some islands of Denmark.

Throughout the trip, I enjoyed the breathtaking scenery and the view of the sea life of a long beach, lush farmland, forests overlooking the fjords, sometimes fishing villages, port cities and of castles. Everything was beautiful with descents of coastal cliffs and dunes.

The dynamic energy of nature overwhelmed me. I felt downright minuscule.

However, there was not enough sun. Many people of color, and whites had to take daily vitamin D tablets for the sun.

During my moments of tranquility, I enjoyed the charm of my private and easy visit by growing in love for Denmark, the Danish language, Danish culture, and the Danes.

Denmark is a Scandinavian country of four hundred islands and fjords in south-western Sweden, south of Norway and bordered to the south by Germany.

It divided Denmark into five regions; The capital region, central Denmark, northern Denmark, Zeeland, and southern Denmark.

The capital is Copenhagen. Danish is the official language. However, many Danes can also speak English, German or French because all Danish students had at least three years of study in English, German or French.

~ Chris B. Missett ~

Danish is one of the hardest languages to learn. Danes do not say, "May I please," they just say, "May I well," (Må jeg godt--) Or you can form a sentence like, "Would you be nice to stop that," for "Please stop that." Sometimes, Gustav, Silije and I, spent our evenings watching TV in Danish and English. It wasn't a problem. We get used to it.

That was my story ... it was my capital sin. Yet, I was an honest teenager. At fifteen and a half, I was not ready to settle anywhere. In any stop in any country, I tried to blend in.

I should have been in high school. The education was very necessary. Shortly, after, I discovered a passion for the Danish school system.

All levels of education in Denmark were free. In addition, even young citizens of foreign nationality could apply for a State Education Grant SU, like Danish citizens.

There were several international high schools in the city where Gustav and Silije lived who offered the International Baccalaureate (IB).

Hosted by Gustav as a tutor, a mentor and by my side, I enrolled in an international high school.

I wanted so much to integrate into Danish society and do the best I could.

Being born in Germany and a citizen of the European Union, I could legally work in Denmark.

I had landed a small part-time job in a private and local airport for aircraft technician training, in a good station specialized for maintenance of the Cessna (Cessna Service Station.)

From time to time, my company tried to put me out of sight because of my young age.

But they limited young people and students to a certain number of hours of work.

I had also tried to integrate myself to the best of my abilities, to do a good job and to make more friends, both at work and in high school.

After my classes, work, and training, Gustav and Silije took me to the streets, clubs, bars, and restaurants several times.

Sometimes we find together useful activities. Sometimes we went fishing too. I loved fishing.

Little by little, I explored the beauty of Den-mark. I wanted to improve my language skills, the Scandinavian culture, and the knowledge of Danish society and even about their ancestors the Vikings.

Most Danish girls and women were blond and had long blond hair or tried to do it. They were kind of very pale because of the northern climate.

I was not a good source of advice on how to woo a Scandinavian girl or woman or any kind.

Maybe, because, of my young age. I was barely sixteen. The chapter of puberty or sexuality was not yet in the book of my life. I was also so shy.

However, my friends Gustav and Silije had introduced me to a young Danish woman about my age named Maja whom I had found intelligent and rather formal.

Gustav, Silije, Maja and I went many times to see great movies of Ingmar Bergman, some of them subtitled in English. Also, many scenes from marriages, even as a teenager when I saw the films: I recognized a profound emotional relationship and the uncomfortable portrayal of spouses as intimate strangers.

Maja had long blond hair and was beautiful. I was wondering why nobody could catch her and keep her. Often, Gustav and Silije joke that Maja and I should be able to marry.

"No," I said often embarrassed. "Our meeting, our courtship was enough — we'll be fine as best friends."

****

Dear Sam,

I miss you, Kelly, Joseph and my mother [...] Sometimes I wake up confused and disoriented!

But, God is creating my roads and taking control of all my fewest obstacles so I can move forward–I feel very safe in his hands.

I always stay with my innkeepers Gustav and Silije. Our friendship began when we picked grapes in Austria and also as traveling companions.

As quickly as we landed in Denmark, they picked up me to their big house. They were sleeping in the master bedroom and I was staying in one of their guest rooms.

Constantly, we have breakfast, lunch, and dinner collectively in the common dining room. I was extremely thrilled.

As a teenager who left his home country abroad, the strange becomes strange.

My friends facilitated my adaptation to life and instilled a sense of myself-confidence.

What a magnificent culture! I enrolled in an international high school for an international baccalaureate (BI.)

I was making new friends, but you knew I was timid. not saying much, also struggling with the new language.

Sam, I grew up a little. On my sixteenth birthday, Gustav and Silije introduced me to their good friend... a young girl. She has a beautiful name: Maja.

I like her a lot. We always try to be part of a group to the best of our ability. Last weekend we caught the ferry and went on a small trip to Sweden.

Cessna hired me for maintenance service plane

checks up, and pilot service.

The main idea was afoot in the door, the work was very exciting, and I was eager.

What I found rewarding about this job was the possibility that I could move to a flying school, perhaps to get a private pilot license.

Sam, I wonder, if you still remember our little secret? You wanted to study medicine to help women with childbirth complications because my biological mother died after giving birth to me?
And I wanted to fly the planes like my dad before he was shot down and killed in Vietnam, also like Bryan, the brother of the Catholic nun our step-uncle, a great airline Pilot in Lufthansa?

Thank you, Sam would give my love to Kelly, Joseph, and my mom?

I love you. I immensely miss you, Sammy.

Love
Delft

12 ~ MADAME DESTINY

With an adventurous spirit, ambitious by nature, I always wanted to learn, and, to network with people from different countries sharing unforgettable moments of lives.

With a free scholarship and education, I am back to campus to accomplish certain of my goals.

The program led to an international Bachelor-degree and the first step to a good aeronautical university in Denmark or in any country.

Further, I had a part-time work which provided ground teaching training for a Certificate of Private Pilot License (PPL.)

In the setup, it was fun going back to school and my part-time work. I was only sixteen yet I was growing independent.

My subjects' programs and work programs were in English followed by Danish's language.

If this might sound unacceptable or dismaying for some people, I wanted to live up to my possibilities and endurance.

Fulfilling my daydreams would be an inspiration by my all struggles and would respond I created it!

In the courses, I often had an assignment done through teamwork. I liked the fact that no one asked me to know everything by heart. Whenever I didn't know or understand something, I could ask somebody and solve the problem.

At my seminars, I had a lot of oral exams sometimes it was difficult to understand the instructor when they translated from Danish. That was the main challenge.

I also was living with my friends who helped me in my studies. Studying in Denmark was a great experience enough and rewarded for me.

Denmark had low crimes, was a wealthy, modern country. The general level of English, German and French amongst the Danes were awesome.

I was living with friends. I had a room and a bathroom. It was a very nice house with a patio where sometimes we ate together and had parties during the summer.

The weather was influencing people's behavior which was surprising. During the summer, people were friendly, outgoing, and happy. The women enjoyed catching a tan.

Many people were thrilled about eating outside. Summer was definitely the time when Denmark and Danes are very open and social.

In the wintertime, people didn't speak much to each other, and they seemed a lot more reserved. They just focused on ongoing homes to light their candles and fireplaces.

Most of the time the weather in Denmark resembled Autumn, Winter, the days were short, cold windy and rainy—those days could become boring supplementing icy nights, discomfort, and sadness.

I liked people at my high school, In the beginning, I felt isolated. Later, when they knew I didn't how to speak Danish.

They didn't bother or judge me; I did not learn Danish yet, but I was a little annoyed as they rarely spoke to me.

Still, I enjoyed listening to them. There was a long way before I could speak or carry a conversation in Danish.

I thought Danes were cautious, so it took a while before deciding, it was credited seeking to learn to see my teammates.

The best experience was after achieving the second semester's exams after I finished my last exam, I joined several of my colleagues at a pub near the campus and we honored the demise of the term.

I was striving with Danish speech and tangling with my timidity. Around 7:30 PM. (19 hr 30), I was solely one non-Dane.

I was contemplating my colleagues talking to each other while we were watching soccer on TV. Boys and girls were yelling for hours together, making placid and friendly request of meaningful chum. It thrilled me to be part of the group.

We drank beer, ate pizza, took pictures and sometimes danced between us. It was a crazy night—a great night; they made several bonds. While everyone shared love except me. I went to my den late.

I had traveled with some other international students in my courses. I met and made some friends at work. That was how to socialize. I also liked the weekend brunch culture.

So many great places for a meal gathering at midday, and so many great cafes with seats outside in the sun we went in. The Danes were very polite and helpful if you asked. They were not proactive about offering help until they got to know you better but once they got to know you; they were very warm people.

It was worth attempting to get to know my Danish colleagues. Most of them were wonderful and friendly people who crossed my life and were much easier and more fun to be around them.

I spent time with my host friends Gustav, Silje, and Maja. They were the ones being referred to as 'friends in need' — they tamed me and became a part of me.

It can be difficult managing the Danish language for some issues.

At last but not least, I believed all the most beautiful women came from Scandinavia!

I threw all I had into studying. After two years of hard study, I received my bachelor degree at the International school and a certificate of Private Pilot License.

They were a meaningful achievement "one in my bucket list!" I said.

The success could have saved me from my life of the Boehme, settle in Denmark or move on with the flow of my fantasies.

Now at least, I had something to show to my biological parents, but my poor mother and father were dead long ago.

I felt so vulnerable to not have someone to whom to show my first achievement.

The void of parents was staggering. I wondered who was watching over me from the firmament, my mother, my father, or God.

"My sweet mother, and gentle father I am getting confused. Have I sinned about leaving my homeland?"

I was squandered here.

"If you please, God, would you forgive me for all my sins I cannot recall," I cried.

The complexity of the different worlds in which we evolve would be a success; success created me a melodrama and a commitment.

Graduation was not my endpoint, but it opened social change so that society could see me through my experiences.

Some questions had reappeared —

Denmark will be a great place. I had already looked for a full-time job, a girlfriend but no plans to get married or have kids any time sooner. Gustav and Silije hosted me, no worries.

In Denmark, I could go beyond graduate school by focusing on the area in which I most wanted to pursue an ambitious career?

Can I return to Germany? How would my family and old friends manage our relationship before and after graduation?

Can I return to Germany? How would my family and old friends manage our relationship before and after graduation?

Some questions had reappeared —

Could I try to discover my father's homeland in the United States — will be much easier? But, in the United States, will I forever as a stranger?

Where should I live? Wasn't I crazy to go looking for my father died long ago?

So, was the parallel of my life? I struggled with doubts and resentments. Feelings of inadequacy began to surface in me.

Madam Destiny...

It may be a dream.
It can be an illusion.
When the paths of glory cross,
open goals, hope, and panic ensue.

Recreating my adventure with each
rising sun the doubt loses its beautiful role.
In the immensity of loneliness without fracture
I sigh; I accept the lessons of my life -

13 ~ THE WORLD OF ILLUSIONS

In the 70s and 80s, to journey in Europe was great, easy and fun. Exploring Europe was the most exciting experience. You layout the whole roads, and countries.

You take luxurious the advantage in the Eu rail following: Austria, Belgium, Bulgaria, Croatia, Czech Republic, Denmark, Finland, France, Germany, Greece, Hungary, Ireland, Italy, Luxembourg, Netherlands, Norway, Portugal, Romania, Slovakia, Slovenia, Spain, Sweden, and Switzerland.

For France, Holland, and Belgium has always attempted to bring all the very best crossings from the continent to the islands of the UK.

Ferries were docking out passing several cities to explore and places to discover. You meet different people, new cultures, new languages, new food and beverages to taste. They were exciting and enriching.

We each of us have at least one other life that unfolds as we travel through the passages of our life— I may call this a parallel life.

We were in June. Since June schools, colleges, and universities were closing their doors.
Summer holidays had begun. Backpackers, boys, and girls were creating adventures offering opportunities.

Whatever this was not a choice for everyone, summer trips were an exciting practical way to enjoy and visit parts of Europe.

I had an ambitious route planned for the next two months and a half, so you'll have lots of time to get to visit the countries of Europe!

→ I created my adventure.

Parts of Europe were exciting to discover, for example; Whether from Copenhagen, Denmark passing to Bonn, and Berlin, Germany, to Amsterdam, Netherlands, to London, England, and Paris, France.

I was adventuring very simple, broadening my horizons and allowing to get to know myself better. Europe was beautiful and inspiring cultures to carry away an excellent opportunity to develop my language skills and...

→ Travel to Bonn and Berlin in Germany

Bonn was the capital of West Germany (GDR) until 1990. People were intrigued by its history, politics, and culture. People located Bonn in the countryside, well served by transport and leisure facilities - Bonn - the hometown of Beethoven.

I stayed in a youth hostel surrounded by the peaceful and gentle countryside of Bonn. Yet a few days after, I watched and enjoyed the multicultural coexistence, the understated atmosphere of the hostel, and the bustling city of Bonn and its romantic surroundings.

I was moved by the city of Berlin, considered the capital of the Nazi Reich, the city divided by the Cold War, Berlin was the capital of East Germany (FRG).

Berlin proved that over time the wounds of world wars could heal, yet the scars remained an important reminder of humanity.

Berliners had worked hard to rebuild their city torn apart by the world wars, but they had also kept shocking memories.

It discouraged anyone when you witness the rest of the wall and check out point Berlin Charlie.

Amazingly, my heart thrilled by the pleasant kindness of Germans people, for their warmth and their affection.

I admired the colorful art on the wall of the Berlin Wall, the East-Side-Gallery. I enjoyed the wonders of the Mauerpark markets, with its variety of street artists that will amuse even the coldest hearts.

→ Travel to Amsterdam, Netherlands

Amsterdam the capital of the Netherlands was a small city with a big personality. Holland known as a great destination for the tourist but has also been as a cheerful country in the world.

Amsterdam, with, houses of nineteenth-century architecture along canals, the city of Amsterdam was a Bicycle culture. Amsterdam proves that good things come in small packages.

I cycled past crooked houses and glanced into the windows to see the doll-house-like coziness of the Dutch.

I sailed along the water canals that give the city of Amsterdam its nickname of 'Venice of Northern Europe' and cruised under sparkling arching bridges.

I did not complete my visit without a peek into the Red-Light District or seeing the works of great Dutch artists, such as Rembrandt and Van Gogh Museum.

I walked most of the time, admiring and learning about some of history's most famous artwork and let Amsterdam inspire me!

→ Travel to London, England

The London, royal capital settled by the Roman Empire. I lived two weeks at the London Meininger hostel Hyde Park was not very expensive for a hostel.

Yet, I wanted to extend my stay in the UK, work was an option. Employment was one of the most practical ways to earn extra money for the summer, and a way to improve my English.

I was with temporary and enthusiastic summer students hired between £10 and £20 an hour for Labor in a dry cleaner.

~ Chris B. Missett ~

My only and first summer's job out of Denmark to allow me to save much of my income without ruining myself.

Whereas, it did not bother me to do the packing, and sorting linen. After the fact, I enjoyed doing simple tasks, and I also made some new friends.

The Tents city was the place that invades you. The Tents city was like a campground, travelers slept in bunk beds under big green tents of the Army.

As the tent's city, the reception, the administration, the showers, the toilets installed in a small building where the pieces of luggage stored in large white luggage bags, closed by a small chain and a padlock.

Tents city was a great summer attraction for teens and young adults. The appealing part of this project was that you could just go there, stay for weeks and weeks or even meet people from any country in the world, without being traveling.

Volunteers from many countries also managed the venue which gave Tents city a friendly, tolerant and lively atmosphere. I went there to play soccer friendly games, scoring many goals against the London boys.

Saturdays, I strolled past Buckingham Palace if so, Her Majesty was at home! I gave her a wave and had a little fun trying to entertain the guards.

I have seen the Tower Bridge, the Palace of Westminster, and the iconic BBC Broadcasting House.

Sometimes I joined the locals unwinding in Hyde Park or ice skating at Hyde-Park Ice rink. I saw the nightlife in Soho, or watch on TV., the spectacular show on West End.

I experienced a few perfects days of sightseeing admiring the Tower Bridge the London Eye, Big Ben, Westminster Abbey and more on.

I spent two months at Tent City. I liked the Tent City. It gave a strange feeling on the last day, to say goodbye to new friends- so many memories!--

But overall, I was satisfied, and the summer was nice in London! A month and a half later jaded, I needed to travel again to spend and enjoy my long break.

I did not want to waste time telling my friends and colleagues in Denmark about my trip, confident that it would impress them.

Still, I had to dash away to the North East of the UK; I headed to Newcastle sail to Amsterdam's destination.

I couldn't help but notice that there was something for everyone but with my Germany Rail Passes, I wanted also to visit France.

→ Travel back to Amsterdam, Netherlands

I sailed along some channels, and under the sparkling bridges that give Amsterdam its nickname "Venice of the North."

My second visit to Amsterdam wasn't cemented without a glance at the red-light district or a walk along the dockyards, wharves, and piers of Amsterdam.

→ The flight From Netherlands to France

Flights from Amsterdam to Paris were low cost. The top Dutch airlines flying to France were KLM. I flew from the Netherlands to France.

From Amsterdam Airport Schiphol, the main international airport of the Netherlands with KLM Airlines.

I arrived in Paris-Charles de Gaulle Airport (CDG) often referred to among the French as Roissy.

But at Paris, Charles De Gaulle international airport, the flight attendant of KLM gave me a boarding pass intended for the next flight on KLM to John F. Kennedy (JFK) International Airport, New York, New York City, USA.

Whoops!!

14 ~ THE WILL OF GOD THE WILL TO WIN

→ Paris, France to New York City, the USA by the Will Divine

I glared at the boarding pass between my fingers. I wanted adventure, now I was seduced by the adventure.

Did I have to take the wrong flight? Can I escape or sneak between the French and American checkpoints of the Transportation Security Administration (TSA)?

I wondered how this could happen to me. Since I had accepted and kept the boarding pass. I had to hitchhike from one plane to another or to become a stowaway?

I needed ability, willingness, and opportunity could I do it? Hurling myself into a difficult situation, could I make the best of it?

The person who hid aboard a plane hoping to get a free passage was a stowaway.

I traveled through most of Europe free and I might as take the risk of being fined or imprisoned since it was illegal in most jurisdictions to embark on aircraft as a stowaway.

I followed the passengers who were lining up to board the large 747 Air France plane bound for New York, in the United States for KLM. I had caught a bad flight. At fifteen, I was fagile and scared.

When our flight left Roissy, France, though, I had changed seats twice because I did not have a seat assigned to me.

The Boeing 747's was a thousand feet of cruising altitude; we were crossing the Atlantic Ocean. The vast stretch waters of the Atlantic, taking up all the parts of the Earth under the plane. I died to see each step of the skyline marked just as the night was chasing the day. It was such a beautiful bird's-eye view!

"Look, remember, I had a valid plane ticket from Paris to New York, with the Alitalia airline in my backpack still, Air France wasn't Alitalia," I said under my breath…

I was contented to see New York, nervous and scared by the outcome of my move. It was a nice and beautiful fight.. it was fears vs. intuition.

We landed at the John F. Kennedy International Airport (JFK). - So be it, I had made my trip to the United States by boarding a passenger plane.

We landed at John F. Kennedy International Airport. That was how I crossed the Atlantic Ocean and made my trip to The United States.

The Kennedy's Airport, the line was moving; I passed in one line... enough, a TSA officer looked at me, then whispered something to his colleague and they started to laugh.

We were in the 70s and 80s. I was not suspicious of any act of terrorism. I was a bold and reckless teenager with no clear goal of violence.

The TSA agent looked at me and asked my name.

"Delft," I said making a show of innocence.

He shook his head, "Are you traveling alone?" He drawled.

I lowered my head, "Yes, sir — I listened in fascination.

"You are United States citizen?"

"Yes, sir — I am a biological child of a U.S. GI."

"Yes? Were you born US citizen?"

"I was born in Germany Sir, in a Caserne Barrack of US's military base."

"And why you come to the US?"

My eyes widened, and my voice trailed off, "My father was a casualty of the US military in Vietnam before I was born. I always wanted to see my father's homeland and North Carolina the birth's state of my father, sir."

He looked at me, "To see the U.S.A. — how long will you stay?"

"Oh... I don't know, sir — is there something wrong?"

"Evidently..."

"What?" I said with a pleading tone.

"I don't know --" the agent shrugged, "I can't imagine what—illegal entry, or what?" he said.

"What they will do to me then?"

"Deport you I guess, sometimes, now there will be a jail sentence," his voice dropped into a whisper, "But only that's if -"

The dark abyss of loneliness swallowed me as far as I missed my family my fantasy faded away instantly.

I winced having second thoughts about the whole search of my American father's relatives living in North Carolina.

I was exhausted and vulnerable, "Oh Lord, I was going to be jailed for illegal entry - I have traveled sometimes illegally non-stop in most European countries and now I'm going to be imprisoned in the United States ... I'll be imprisoned for illegal entry - but - I'm legally minor," I said, making a great show of innocence.

My show was both instinctive and absurd like a schoolboy in trouble.

"Oh, yes, illegal entry, vagrancy, and moping around of course, you will be interviewed first," he said hesitantly.

~ Chris B. Missett ~

I was terrified and sad. Unexpectedly, silent tears started to soak my shirt.

After realizing the confusion, John F. Kennedy International Airport (JFK) stated that KLM had coordinated efforts with the Air France airline to provide a return flight to Paris, and then offered me two nights at a hotel near Kennedy International Airport (JFK). A TSA agent will be by my side.

Everything seemed strange. I was in the United States. The sounds, the voices, and people were speaking different English from the British English— the language American English.

I was so scared that a torrent of tears flowed, repeatedly, on my bruised cheeks. However, I could not wait to see New York and discover the wonders of a great metropolis of the United States and the world.

The second night, because I had enough money to support myself, knew English although I did not have a passport or an entry visa, but being a child abandoned by a US veteran passed away and by divine will, the Security Administration allowed me to enter the United States without "notice of appearance" at an immigration court on a certain date.

I wanted so much to see Disney World. I bought a return ticket with Greyhound to go to Orlando, Florida. I arrived in Orlando, after the tour at Disney, Sea World, and "Yeah Cap Kennedy!"

As I had not yet got a visa or US citizenship, I supported myself with a few unskilled jobs most of the times farm and seasonal work.

.

15 ~THE USA WAS BEAUTIFUL BUT ALSO A THEATRE OF MISERIES

Even though, the tide of time led me to Orlando, Florida, I thought I should conquer my dreams. Daydreams enticed me with the start of the fall.

I tried to enroll at Embry Riddle Aeronautical University in Daytona Beach, Florida. But, the high tuition drained my illusions and my dreams. The discomfort invaded me.

The difference between the cultures and the traditions from state to state frightened me and seemed to create me an immense fear of the unknown and not ambushed by cultural dogmas.

The fear of failure vs. embarrassment became significant between me and my peers.

The language barrier was a frustrating hurdle. I kept struggling to learn English and little by little to allow me to mingle in society so much dreamed of.

The first year in the United States had a negative impact.

But, as time passed, I made a multiple-choice of inspiring heroes for my moral courage and inner peace in myself. Such as the persistence of Mahatma Gandhi, who led a pacifist revolution to end British rule in India.

The British put Gandhi in prison; he fasted until he was as thin as a bone-thin to control his destiny.

The assassination of John F. Kennedy also found a place in the collective mind. JFK had an aura! His loss disheartened American families and young and old people around the world.

The aerospace, Wernher Von Braun was a German and American aerospace engineer and space architect, and John Herschel Glenn the pilot, engineer, astronaut, senator and first American to orbit the Earth. Just as, I visited the Kennedy Space Center and touched the capsule in which John Glenn journeyed around the Earth.

Even, if I did not have yet American citizenship, I began to wo
.rk full time as a seasonal farm worker.

16 ~ BLINDING IN

We meet ... we talk ... we laugh
Then we go our separate ways,
and yet that is not enough.

Your smile echoes like
a piece of music in my heart.
A strange attraction is intensifying.

Again, we meet, we talk, we laugh.
Then we go our separate ways;
However, that's enough.

Feelings of tenderness grow
Captivating and more beautiful,
Please do not ask me if I love you [...]

It was funny. Thoughts of love faded away, but, her memories kept appearing in my heart.

People talk about falling in love. I did not fall in love. I grew in love with Rose. I met Rose seems like a dream. What kind of woman is Rose now? A woman who makes everyone happy?

Rose was a college girl and I was a vaga-bond. When recollections and visions of Rose come back to haunt me from time to time, sometimes I feel hopeless about my life.

It was funny. Thoughts of love faded away, but, her memories kept appearing in my heart, people talk about falling in love. I did not fall in love. I think I grew in love with Rose.

Strange, how memories of a long-ago friendship can be so present in my heart. I meant not to meet Rose; a fateful a coincidence it was alike.

One evening, a group of boys and girls from Messiah College came for church services at the Mission. The 'Mission' was a covenant house for runaway children and a few transients.

At the 'Mission': I was helping some children on the run. The evening was tranquil.

When the services and the dinner ended, it was all about the Gospel, the best way for Christian students, to meet runaway children.

The college group came to share Church's teachings. Students used their testimonies of their faith to evoke empathy for the runaway children.

The runaways exhibited both depravity and innocence. I liked that evening. I knew as a Catholic, a little about the Gospel outside of what they wrote in the Missal.

I sat alone in the corner. A girl across from me met my glance and advanced towards me with a smile.

Hi there…my name is Rose," she said as she sat next to me. How are you? How long have you been here?"

Oh, just ignore me. What do you want to know? Then an innocent feeling awoke in me. I… I'm a vagabond, I said to myself under my breath.

"Hmm, why should I care about?" I frowned at her.

Her hazel eyes ablaze with friendliness looked at me. She smirked, "Don't you think someone cares where you from are?"

"I'm from my mother, I do not know anymore if the love I get from good people is not just an act of pity," I said snubbing her.

I wanted to know her. Someone wanted to strip away my innocence or wanted to change me.

But, when I looked at Rose, she grinned. "Well, I know that we all do." She teased.

"I grew up in Western Europe," my words trailed off, as my eyes becoming more vacant than they already were.

I looked was born in East Germany, my mother was born in West Germany, and..." She paused reaching for words.

"You are from Germany too?" I interrupted.

She stared at me at Rose, and, I wanted to create her joy to find me.

"I'll be OK someday," I told her. "I like some-times to be alone. It is pleasant."

Rose smiled without looking up at me, her deep-dimples on her rosy cheeks reflected her sensitivity, "My father was born in East Germany, and my mother was born in West Germany, and," She paused reaching for words.

"Are you from Germany?" I interrupted.

She stared at me, with a smirk and shook her head from side to side.

"No, I am from New Jersey," she said, giving on me one of her candid smiles. Her smile stroked me. It felt like the first caress of warm waves on my feet after a long winter.

"My name is Delft. They stationed my parents at an American military base in West Germany. I was born there." I continued, "I lived my childhood there, and when I was six years old, I went to a Catholic boarding school in France, I also lived in France for seventeen years."

"How did you end up at the Mission, Delft?"

"You think all runaways children are the same, some college students like you who have no worries will never know."

"What do you mean? What opportunity can you get without a college degree?"

"Of course not, college is not for everyone. But I can try, OK?"

Rose looked as though she hurts for me. We sat silently for a few moments. I'll never forget that meek and empathy looks on her face. I was surprised. As we sat there, guiltless tears began to fill my eyes.

"I'm sorry," she said. "You still have time. You just think about it more."

"No worries. I'll be OK. I do not need any friends." I said.

"How do you know how the way I feel? You just meet me."

"Well, I would like to share Christ with the other boys!" Rose's voice changed to a meekly sweet one.

"Oh, O.K," I sighed and watched her as she walked away.

A few minutes later, a voice came from one corner.

"Oh, well, guys it's about time to go!" The voice belonged to the leader of the group.

Rose tore her eyes from the other boys and turned her gaze to me, sending to me flashes of kindness and trust.

"Sorry," she said. "You still have time. Just think about it more."

"Goodbye Delft, I'll be praying for you." Rose waved at me.

I enjoyed and appreciated Rose's tenderness.

"Goodbye Rose." I smiled back at Rose.

As I recall, the understanding of the Gospel drifted throughout the room. Everyone had lost that defensive shell that people wear until they're sure they can trust someone.

Then, after the students left, I moved on down two rows of seats into a dark corner of the room. I looked away. For that night I engulfed myself into a distance. Without moving, I soared miles away far beyond the room.

I splashed into sketches of memories. I had a whole range of memories: recollections of memories of challenge, courage, and pride.

It came to pass that the child in me dripped into the memory of walking out of the Catholic boarding house.

The Catholic boarding house was the stand-in family that had adopted me.

Feelings of self-reproach kept me running away. "I had a pleasant childhood in the boarding house, but, I felt abandoned by my biological parents. Often I was in pain and resentful of myself because of the absence of a father and mother. I was alone."

In the silence's desert, I listened to echoes of the years I spent in Europe. Stretching in my mind shades of those reminiscences overlapped and unfolded like a drama. I daydreamed. Drunk with anguish or ecstasy, I listened to the nostalgic visions.

My choice had become my capital sin. It became the trade of my life. Feelings were part of my life. Sometimes I yearned for love and for a gentle acceptance...acceptance that I could value. Sometimes my daydreams were mere fantasies.

I was a silent adventurer in a romantic quest for adventure and bright destiny. My first years on the chase of fate were an agony of homesickness, nostalgia, guilt, and sorrow.

Off and on, I had vague fears of emptiness, fears of being very lonely and feeling fragile. I never set out to make friends. I did not object to making friends. But, I wasn't trying for any.

Some days I thought I needed friends. Some days it was only adding resentment to it. As I realized my loneliness, I just lived in delusion, pretending that someday I would meet a friend who will say, I want to know you — your strengths and your faults. And I will accept you anyway.

Rose was a college sophomore. She was tall, thin and pretty. She had strawberry blond hair and translucent peach skin. When she well dressed, she looked like a model.

Some people would call her a snobby girl. She was a desirable person, with a great ability to make friends.

Rose's parents sent her to private school, urging her to get a college degree and great career. But, more than that, she was a beautiful girl.

Rose and I met by chance. We were strangers among strangers, each carrying a mystery within us — the unknowable mystery of our feelings of the heart and of being.

But she liked me. My overwhelming emotion at that point was only respect, which that melted into genuine Christian love.

She was into different leagues...I liked her without knowing why. It was like blind fate and blind feelings.

Two weeks passed. The group came again. This time as soon as the services ended, Rose, who was with a girlfriend, scanned the crowd for my face.

She and her girlfriend found me for a friendly hug, "This is my friend, Delft..."

Rose's eyes met mine, each one wondering what we would discover in the other, a friend or a foe, a supporter or an opponent.

"Hi, how are you?" Rose's girlfriend greeted me.
"I'm fine,"
Rose waved me to seat down by me, she and her girlfriend both sat next to me. She nudged me in the leg and said,
"Hey, do you have a Bible?"
"Bible!--" I acknowledged with condescension in my voice, as an atheist might reply to a Christian who has talked to him about his beliefs in God. I want people to stay out of my problems.

"Yes, a Bible." Her eyes held mine, as she smiled, "I thought so, a daily Bible reading enriches your spiritual life. I brought you one."

I was startled at what I saw, a very beautiful Bible. Then, I was humiliated and stunned. I blushed with embarrassment. I accepted the Bible.

"Thank you very much." I glanced at her. I could not hold back any longer my satisfaction. "If you please, let's do this, could you sign it for me?"

Rose and I exchanged smiles.

"Sure!"

She touched my shoulder and wrote:

Praise the Lord for our friendship. You helped me in my walk with the Lord and I will pray that you continue to help others too. I will pray that the Lord will guide you in your walk and that you will always turn to him.

Rose

What she had written surprised me a lot. When she smiled at me, and, in the Bible, there was an epitaph a poem about friendship. The poem reads:

~ Weep, to a Beloved Destiny ~

Friendship…

A friend is like a tower strong,
A friend is like a joyous song.
That helps us on our way.

A friend is like a tower strong.
A friend is like a joyous song.
That helps us on our way.

When the golden ties of friendship
Blind the heart to heart,
Mind to mind, how fortunate are we!

For friendship is a noble thing;
it soars past death,
on Angel's wings to eternity.

God bless friendship,
holy bond both here
and in the great beyond

a benefit priceless.
Then may we know
that wondrous joy.

That is precious
Or without alloy;
The friendship based on Christ.

About the middle of reading the poem, pledge of our friendship, I felt the message in me. I did not know how to explain it. An audible voice she said, she's a friend.

I conversed with God Almighty God, would it be possible for Rose to become my friend? Knowing this is not an easy request, but I would be grateful. Thank you, Father Celeste. It was more like a dream than reality.

I knew it. But Rose was next to me and was talking to me. Reflecting on it, I wondered if it was a prayer. She was like a sequence of a dream, and I trapped in why and how.

Why is she kind to me? I am a fugitive, looking for a normal life again. She is so pretty and well dressed. Why should she care about me? Destiny must be blind. She called me "friend". She gave me a Bible ... me. Did she feel pity or empathy? The feelings must be blind.

I was moving away from my nice house. What I needed most was an opportunity to change my destiny. I was an orphan. Rose was a college student. She and I had different friends. She and I, came from different social classes. Different lives, different ideas, and different backgrounds.

She shared now a small part of her perfect world with me. I wondered what people would say about such a set of opposites appeared free in real life.

We became friends little by little. I thought my life was interchanging. It was a feeling of friendly comfort and compatibility.

Rose introduced me to his friends. I felt however; I felt very unworthy. She in all her abilities had made me acceptable.

However, when I was a child, my first ambition was to be an aeronautical engineer or test pilot. For, at seventeen, I had my private pilot license and attended a college in Denmark.

Knowing that Rose sacrificed to me her own caring love, I was thirsty for her sincere love. That's how I started thinking about going back to school ...

I longed to be part of Rose's friends. Resorting to my daydreams and wondered how I could use her college life to implement my goals.

I recall times as a child; my first ambition was to be an aeronautical engineer or a test pilot. By seventeen I had my private pilot's license and was attending college in Denmark.

Thinking Rose was sacrificing her pure, cherish, and affection for me, I enjoyed for her sincere friendship. I commenced to realize; I was going back to educate myself...

17 ~ COMMITTED TO A FATE

It was Jun, a year after I met Rose. Yet English as a second language, I passed the SAT test at Princeton University in New Jersey.

The coming fall, I enrolled at Wilson College in major computer science. I liked my classes.

Inspired by Rose's intentions, I controlled my first year of college. Rose had developed into part of my creative envisage, and my unending mentor.

~ Weep, to a Beloved Destiny ~

During the Seasons Holidays' break, Rose was going home to her parents. "Well, Delft, come meet me after Christmas, my parents demand to greet you," Rose said on the phone with a friendly voice.

Somehow, meeting Rose's family struck me.

"Rose, come on, I know you are joking!" I spoke to her from a telephone booth. "You tell them I am in adventurer status?"

"I'm not that stupid! Do you think the best way to create the first impression would be to say? The boy is an adventurer?" She continued, "Apart from that, he is fine. I told them you were a nice, normal boy and that they would enjoy meeting you."

"I don't want to…" I began, when she cut me off.

"I am asking you if you really care about me," I breathed a long breath, "Please, Rose."

"Delft, listen," she begged, "Please, are sure you don't want to come home with me for the Holidays?"

"Please what? Your parents will be disappointed later they get to know me."

"I've told them all about you. They do not have it. They want to see you… um; would you be my…Guess who's coming to Dinner? Rose cackled.

"Yeah right — oh sure, you're on your own, there," I acknowledged.

In unison, we both laughed at each other. The pleasant part was applicable.

"I am not coming… besides, I wouldn't be part of your household, and I don't want to crowd your parents. I don't want folk feeling sorry for me."

She laughed then, "Please, Delft, we've become good friends. You are a decent person. It's made them want to see you. You ought to be charmed. Come on. I'll come to pick you up at the supermarket close to my house."

"Yeah right," I grunted again and hung up.

It was strange. But, I was excited about the idea that Rose had invited me. I get excited that she was the one who swept me along without giving me time to refuse.

I got nervous. This girl's parents saved money to send her to college to learn. Now she was to bringing home an adventurer.

Should I cancel it for her sake? But, it would be better to show up…better manners and for the good of our friendship, it was something best to do.

I went, much against my will, complaining that I had no wish to speak about my running away. But before I got close to the house, I bought a bottle of white French wine for her parents and a pretty bouquet for Rose.

"Delft, thank you for coming…" Rose called to me.

"And thank you, Rose, for asking me."

"Was it easy to find your way up here?"

"Thanks, you gave me good directions."

Rose and I met a few blocks away from her house at a supermarket. When I got there, I called her to come to pick me up.

It was a nice house with a swimming pool in the yard. Rose ran ahead as if she feared I might think better of it. She put her finger on the bell and kept it there.

"You look surprised," she said laughing.

"No." I blushed. "It just doesn't look like you."

"Well, let's go in. I'll introduce you to my parents."

"Coming…coming," an accented voice said. I thought it might be her father.

When I arrived at Rose's parents' house, the door opened just as I indoors breathless on the landing, Rose peered into the house with a big smile fixed on her lips.

"Dad, here's my friend, Delft," Rose said in a tone I did not care for, as if she was here in a game of tennis.

I humbly said, "Good morning, sir."

Very reserved, and shy, I held out my hand to Rose's father.

He manly grabbed it, imprisoned it. "You are Delft. I'm David, Rose's father," he said attentively and gently drew me into the house where Rose previously fled.

"Good morning, Delft — I'm Greta," a female voice with a strong German accent greeted me.

As I regained possession of my hand from the father, I turned in her direction. Greta was the mother.

Rose's mother appeared, detaching herself from the kitchen. She was a quiet, kind woman with blond hair, and she wore a long dress.

"Mother, this is Delft," Rose said, looking at Greta with a small smile as they stood in front of me.

The mother put out her hand, just as her husband did. I shook her hand.

Rose's parents were superb. I did not know what to expect, but our first meeting went. Rose's father asked me the usual questions about Europe, school, trying to understand the curious place where his daughter and I had met.

Her mother looked at my face and made polite conversation about Rose. It was a pleasant meeting, and we had a pleasant luncheon meal.

"Maybe you'll come to see us again," Rose's father said.

Rose didn't tell enough, but it affected me how wonderful she was like her mother.

I saw how she had picked up to be so gentle and kind. She was like her friends, but she was like her parents too.

I was startled at the range of conflicting emotions I felt for Rose. The excitement, the attraction, the respect, trust, fear, distance, and closeness: all at once. At the end of the introduction, Rose had to drag me away.

"You look so surprised, Delft." Rose was amused, and she laughed.

"No, I just saw in you something very different from what you are when you are with your friends."

"For real, Delft," Rose smiled.

"Yes… sort of."

Rose's cheeks blushed with pleasure. "Do you like them, Delft?"

"I enjoyed meeting them. Meeting your parents makes our friendship worthwhile."

I was frankly touched. I did not know what to say to Rose.

Driving on my way home from Dumont New Jersey to the Wilson College campus in Chambersburg Pennsylvania. I kept thinking about the moments I spent at Rose's house with her family.

I changed and set up to grow into enamored of Rose's nature. She was special. Reasoning about being on the adventure, I found out why I had not called to go there.

I cried for a family; I cried for a home. A rush of anger scorched through me. It was partly angered at me, for I well knew that I was on the run, and the session wound down to the wistful words of John Lennon:

When I find myself in times of trouble
Mother Mary comes to me.
Speaking words of wisdom let it be, let it be.

Rose and I were drowning in a beautiful and innocent relationship. She started to hang out more frequently with me. Pleasurable and powerful sets of memories of Rose fascinated and haunted me.

Until then my fondest recollections, the absolute pinnacle of intimacy was having lunch with Rose's family on the day of her graduation.

While at the luncheon given by her father in a very fancy restaurant, Rose hesitated, not sure where I would sit. Girlishly, Rose's fourteen-year-old niece Christina pulled out the chair on Rose's left wanting to sit next to her. Rose looked disturbed. She half rose from her chair, "No, Christina, let Delft sit next to me." She gently smiled at her.

Her tone was low, and she realized immediately what she had made. I remained to stare at Rose for a while, feeling a delicate pleasure in her, as if I were her achievement.

There was a short silence around the table, and Rose's dad David, and her mom Greta, looked at her, and then took in the rest of the family around the table with one glance. Then the conversation began again. I was impressed by Rose's family.

At my side, I was thinking, I just cannot believe that God gives us lovable people in our lives and then asks us not to love them. I was full of the memory of Rose and her family. So, I was growing fond of Rose.

******

"I thank you," I said sitting to her left side.

Rose's father took a picture of us. Rose's mother hugged me and invited me to help Rose move off-campus. They all treated me just like a member of the family. When we were ready to leave the Messiah campus, Rose kissed my cheek friendly:

"Well, maybe you'll come to see me in New Jersey one day."

"Thank you, Rose," I looked into Rose's eyes for a long time and then held out my hand to shake hers.

"You bet," Rose leaned toward me and gave me another kiss on my cheek.

After, I became a college student, leaping from the old into the new life, connecting the dream to my heart, I wanted to have the best grades, the best education, and even attend the best graduate school, to create a binding tie between Rose and me.

I was Rose's creation. People say: "That college or university graduation is the best student."

As if, with Rose, graduation also came the end of our friendship.

Rose. She was moving back to New Jersey and getting married to a high school sweetheart. Then two years and a couple of weeks slipped by after I visited Rose for the holiday season and, I found a letter in my mailbox. The letter was a brief letter:

> *Dear Delft,*
> *I guess that we will never see each other again. My parents and I are going back to Germany. I will stay there. Please, Delft, make me proud.*
> > *Love*
> > *Rose*

I read that letter twice. Then my heart sank. She said she was going with her parents, but I did not know why they had to leave. And not come back.

A feeling of coldness frightened me and lay all over me. I started to cry silent tears. I knew that I would never see her again. It was strange to think that we would never again speak to one another.

I smiled at the memories and I wondered why the curtain had to close, leaving me on an empty stage. I wrapped my arms around myself and wept.

As I thought of our relationship, dreams of Rose flooded by the knowledge she was flying out of my life. I sighed with a sudden stab of pain, "So that's farewell, Rose. Our friendship was the most natural and most wonderful thing in my life. I grew in love with you, but I will never see you again."

I regretted picturing her leaving me and finding a new friend.

I will not wipe our friendship out by changing life; I will go through everything from you, even if your affection for me becomes cold or dies.

> *For, you've given me the gift,*
> *of the truth of your openness.*
> *For, you've shown me*
> *how much you care.*
> *You are a special friend.*
> *I love you more, and*
> *more with each passing day.*

I wanted to live; I would begin a new life. However, I kept careful track of the time since I'd see Rose, fishing from memories to torture myself. I wished it was only a dream. But, one month, two months…one year: the endless wait was tearing me apart. Then, I stopped counting. I was coming to terms with the idea that Rose was a person of special value and a friend who liked me enough to become my best friend. Still, I missed her in my busy life.

The pain of being in love with, Rose was excruciating, it was burying me. As the days passed, depression crept over me I feared no longer did I journey through the days expected of her presence.

No longer did I sense wholeness within me. Dear heaven, please look after Rose.

I felt a mild bout of anxiety. I will not cry…I will not. But, I felt hurting tears rush into my eyes, and a lump formed in my throat. Rose, adieu, the brown, girlish eyes, and the blond hair.

I drew a fountain of memories - sat inside it, and wondered whether Rose, too, was sucked under by the whirlpool of feelings that swirled within me.

How, will I ever survive alone? I sought escape in my emptiness, in my studying, and in my writings to feed my lonely brain, keeping my GPA above 3.50. Before I become conscious of it, the second year at Wilson College and my graduation were before me.

While, at my graduation, in my college uniform for the commencement, I wanted to give a phone call to Rose with the news that "I was graduating." Wherever, I never did that day. Halfheartedly, what was the point of celebrating if Rose couldn't be there, and we would never see each other again?

My celebration was a mixture of nostalgia, warmth, and slight anxiety because I had been accepted at Drexel University, a four- year's college and a top university in the United States, in Philadelphia.

The fall following my graduation, from Wilson College in Chambersburg, a small town, I was transferring to Drexel University, in Philadelphia, the biggest city in Pennsylvania for a four years college degree.

While, in Philadelphia, I waded through illusions of yesterday's…I thought of Rose. My feelings set aside like a worn toy, to escape studying seemed my only way out of my sorrows.

During, my first year at Drexel, I fell in love with the red bricks of an Ivy League School. The University of Pennsylvania (UPENN), with its Wharton School number 1 of the School of Business of the world, a great place for an MBA…

I signed up for two summers at U-Penn School of Engineering. I took computer science courses besides my full load of classes at Drexel University.

Being in Philadelphia most of my days filled with heavy pieces of solitude, studying and creative writing became the supplies for and the excitement of my hermitage life, the idiotic life of a hermit.

Love left me, the passing infatuation has gone. I felt as if I was carrying a load on my shoulders.

My Thrill had faded away. I was all alone, for all I cared was to be alone with the pain of my compassionate love for Rose. Killing my feelings for Rose was a way to suppress my sorrow and emptiness.

I spent hours at the library, the computer center, and even at the ice-skating rink, trying to block the sorrows of Rose's leaving, which was cutting my soul at its deepest point.

Well, isolated, I withdrew deeper and deeper into myself, trying to figure out what I could trust as love. I pleaded, please Rose save me.

> *I feel abstract...*
>
> *Thinking of you,*
> *sweet feelings of appreciation*
> *fill my mind.*
> *In the serenity of your absence,*
> *my heart speaks to you without words ...*

Many months of silence passed. There, was no word of her. Then, Rose broke my isolation again with a letter:

> *Dear Delft,*
>
> *Well, many changes have occurred in my life. I keep asking how you are doing. Please, write and*

~ Weep, to a Beloved Destiny ~

let me know. I want to give you my dreams….
Delft, make me proud.

Love
Rose

Once, again, I imagined that the differences between our lives and the birth of our relationship seemed to disappear. It was a dream I wanted to dream a little longer.

Rose, why, would you continue to appear in my heart? My new social change is all about you.

We all had dreams. We realize some while others are nothing but dreams. I thought I would not have that kind of dreamlike Rose's dream and me.

I was thankful to Rose for sharing her intimacy. I was indebted to Rose because I knew her meeting had helped me change. For, new friends and old friends often disappear. There will be one day, a marriage, a home, a family, new interests and new values. I frowned for not to cry.

As the echoes of remembrances washed up like waves in my ears, I looked back There reflected a charming taste of recognition. Rose was in Germany.

She was not conscious sufficient for me to tell her the words I would prefer to express:

> *I am overwhelmed because I encountered you.*
> *At the journey of our friendship,*
> *Your qualities allowed influencing my life*
> *Thank you, for you have been my confidant...*

A little lonely, sad, and scared, and with nostalgia and warmth, I listed my visions of Rose.

A good dream, the pride, or the folly, ever so beautiful feelings of Rose will linger in my yearning.

Rose came closest to my fantasies and my dreams. I kept wondering if, from the day I was born, someone destined me to meet Rose. She led me with courage.

Rose changed my strange adventure and my terrible sadness, she made my passion. With, remembrances came new confidence from an adventurer to a college student or an Ivy League university student.

Maybe missing Rose created the opportunity for me to become the main character and my fate to form life in the American mainstream. Since I found a unique heroine in Rose, I treasured those times with her in my heart.

Maybe I honestly loved Rose. Maybe I always will. But, once upon a time, someone said: "Nothing lasts forever. Yet, for those who love with heart and soul, there was no such thing as separation and no sorrows like separation."

I gave Rose recognition, for she gave me perfect friendship. I praised her for creating my whole life. My future will ever apply to Rose.

I started to fall in love with the best universities in the Northern United States. One summer I attended the Johns Hopkins, at Homewood for the engineering.

The following summer, I transferred to the University of Maryland, College Park, for software engineering.

The next year, they accepted me at both Cornell University, in New York, and the University of Utah, in Salt Lake City, to study engineering and medical informatics. I opted myself transferring to The University of Utah.

The world seemed to me like a huge maze. What if I lost my direction again and walked?

Well, my sin climbed up a ladder that I should not climb. I strived for the best in my higher education until I woke up from my dream. I will probably be thankful for my life for someone like Rose or looked like Rose was just another stop on my destiny.

> *In the fullness of my life...*
> *I've constantly good dreams,*
> *I even named wonderful.*

Fanciful dreams of long, long ago,
dream of how my fate should be.

In the reckless moments,
I want to keep on dreaming of my destiny.
I silently speak to my dreams.
I linger in the good ones.

Softly as my dreams murmur among themselves,
some raptures fade away and lessen their glow.
Some dreams recoil. Their regrets retort to me.

I shy away from those ones, unable to appreciate
such happiness again, alone, and contemplative,
I breathe a deep breath drinking my anguish.

I was partly livid and depressed because I had a few hard things to tell what I had to tell. In the beginning, I was very excited to be in the USA. Living in such a great country was ma chance to enhance my social settings.

Enduring and working will help me to grow into maturity and cultivate my life. But, I never thought that I will miss home, my siblings, my friends, even Europe that much:

Dear Mom,

I don't think it was a good idea that I crossed the Atlantic Ocean and came to the USA.

The country itself is so beautiful. You can marvel at its cities, fascinating history.

The appreciation of the immersion culture, the homeless people sharing the secret side of those *loveable* cities also makes the USA a theatre of miseries.

I am still looking forward to visiting my died father's native state, North Carolina and also perhaps his living relatives. But it might also be a culture shock.

Meantime, I will be extremely busy with my higher education. I started a post graduated program in a college of software engineering.

So dear mom, home was only making me feel more nurtured and connected. Have a little faith in me

Love
Delft.

18 ~ WEEP, TO A BELOVED DESTINY

It was in autumn. The night was beautiful and starry... Through, my window, I scanned the milky way as if I were looking into a deep bottomless well when the full moon hanging from the sky had broken my serenity.

At first, I thought the full moon would follow its usual trajectory in the sky. But, she woke up my innocent destiny.

Then, a passionate desire for a new freshness of night-life was unfolding. As I smiled, my window brightened, and the Moon came closer to me and whispered, "Make a wish --"

"Huh, is this a wish game?" I asked.

"Well, when people stare at me, they like to make wishes."

"Do I have to?"

"You should tell me what wishes do you have."

"Well, you pretty and sparkling Moon, just shine and leave me alone."

"I am positive — you have a wish!"

I yawned, "Splendid," I hummed, "Is this the desire of the Heavens?" Then I exhaled, "Do you always ask people to make a want? Just stroll in the hollow sky."

"Just create a wish. How many are there? Are you afraid that your wishes will make you feel stupid?"

"Um…what do I do, then? It is the same thing. Do you think something good might happen to me tomorrow? Or you just want me to feel better?" I forced myself to answer.

"When someone wants something very much, he/she will do everything; for it. And you are not exempt from that."

"I mean nothing to you; all my wishes stay imputed in my heart." I passed up at the Moon.

"Make a wish — make a wish — make a wish…"

"Please, do not tease me. I do not want to challenge you. I am just human. Humans are emotional beings, which is why humans have feelings. Many times I have become attached to those who once showed compassion or empathy to me, those who cared for me, those who loved me…or even to those who love for the love of God. But, I always rely on Jesus to look for hope and rest. This world is a strange place to be. The world changes — people change. Even love has a force that can make love change."

"Sometimes you should live to be positive! Don't you have a family?" the capricious Ms. Moon asked.

My mind asked my heart, and my inner child sighed, these days of my childhood gone by the time I left home.

"Do I have precious memories of a family? All I have is empty yearning for family […]"

"Your family…?" the Moon insisted.

"Oh, well, I am depressed of the wisdom of making yearns to you. Do I have a family — hum a family that wishes happiness for each other…a well-beloved family?"

"It is okay, even if you do not live together now."

"Oh, that kind of family? Well, it is okay even we don't live together now? Even if, we think of each other as family now, then we are still a family?" I asked.

"Does everyone have a family?"

"Even someone like me?" I shrugged.

"Yes."

"And, what about you, have you lost your parents too? Because you're always alone in the sky?" and I continued, "Me, I always believed that I had the best family ever...a few brothers and sisters older than me, I could look upon. But those brothers and sisters are not here anymore. I am not a bad or a good person, but I am being punished by being alone, all alone."

Then, a dull sarcasm spread over the Moon's face darkened.

"Maybe you just hide behind your loneliness all the time," Ms. Moon said.

"Beautiful full Ms. Moon, I'm not sure, I do not allow wailing in my life. If, I stare at you, and the sky, many stars look like eyes, I drown old good remembrances into a silence. I have been too long without family. Does my family look at me? A family now is just but a word. My parents are dead if you are looking at them; my mother and my father are you looking at me now? Whenever I am melancholy, I cry for you, I miss you now. Miss Moon, if you please, tell them I always think of them? Can they forgive me for sulking?" There, I sighed and tears overfilled my eyes:

My mother for giving me birth,
for exchanging your own life me:
I still feel your maternal arms around me.
Invisible, but you are always present.
I will always love you to infinity,
my sweet and tender mother I love you ..."

"Maybe, you appropriate with solitude because of your knowledge?" Ms. Moon asked.

"Why do you summon me such a situation — do you want to die? I experience my pain and my sorrows through desolation. To welcome to be alone is that, to be conceited to my breakdowns?"

"I am watching your troublesome events. You should rise on your two feet and that's why you came to this world."

"Oh, this world is a field of thorns, and the eyes of people can undermine strength!" I complained.

"Just make a wish -- what is your next wish? I give you the whole wide sky. Yet you were born with a fate."

"Milky-Moon, do you care if it is a lie? I have grown more and more resentful about my childhood."

"Why is that?" "Oh, this world is a field of thorns, and the eyes of people can undermine strength!" I complained.

"Just make a wish — what is your next wish? I give you the whole wide sky. Yet you were born with a fate."

"Oh, this world is a field of thorns and the eyes of people can undermine strength," I complained.

"Milky-Moon, do you care if it is a lie? I have grown more and more resentful about my childhood."

"Because; of my childhood dreams. One, I wanted to have a good education and be with the best travel and live in different places, and through the course of mon voyage, to experience diverse people and cultures while exploring the depths of the human experience. Maybe my parents did not want to stand by my hard times --"

"I do not want to stir up your old memories. You have a good education, and you have been too many places. How did you come so far?"

"I came so far with the strength of my heavy solitude."

"You came so far with the strength of solitude?" she echoed.

"Yes. Solitude is a kind of strength, as is the fear vs. intuition, and the Will of God." I answered.

"So, you cannot cross that field alone? Aren't you able to control your destiny?"

"Well, the world changes, people change, and life is so perplexing. I don't want to blame the others, either. I want to suffer my heartbreaks and failures in quiet. Therefore, I just wore the coat of the orphanage passively since I abandoned my family -- and became an orphan." I said loudly.

"I have no father.
I have no mother.
my parents play hide and seek with me.
I have no one to love."

"Your parents were contented when they gave birth to you. You made it. Having life is a win!"

It embarrassed me to look at her, I shed a silent tear.

"Do you want to die?" I said, "Well, I suppose my family ties will never change till I die. Maybe being on my all alone is the way to atone for my sins."

"And, what about your next wish?"

"Hey, Miss Moon, do you know that you are the queen of passion and deceit?"

The Moon fascinated stared at me from a piece of the sky,"I am?"

Well, people change…even love has fierceness, and can change."

"Have they have hurt you?" The Moon asked.

"Nobody is immune to feelings. But it seems like love always accompanied by both happiness and sorrow. I'm fine, writing helps me to identify feelings of pain and sorrow, and to put a pane of glass to the window of memories. When emotions linger long, sometimes, I can express my appreciation." Silly me, I thought.

"Is that so?"

"Yes, Miss Moon."

With a shy smile, I glanced at the Moon, and at my words, the rascal Miss Moon sparkled even more.

"Make a wish to someone." She grinned.
"Are you so influential or what?" I asked.

At my words, the full Moon sparkled and winked at me.

"You're so boyish!"
"If you please — be nice missy!" I said.
"Come on, make a wish I will be your messenger," she repeated.
"No—" I laughed. "Wait, a minute — If you please, do not confuse me. I always like stories and fairy tales. But — they are scary."
"Why would you?"
"Well… Miss Moon, why people make promises they don't intend to keep? Instead of saying *'Goodbye'* they say, *'See you later'*, and the only thing they knew about each other was perhaps their names. – chances are, they will never see each other again, don't you think so?"
"Hum — I think so!" Miss Moon said.
"And don't you feel lonely sometimes? Have you had any parents, brothers, or sisters?" I asked her with a silly smile.
I laughed. "Wait, a minute — If you please, do not confuse me. I always like stories and fairy tales. But — they are scary."

"Why would you?"

"Well… Miss Moon, why people make promises they don't intend to keep? Instead of saying 'Goodbye' they say, 'See you later', and the only thing they knew about each other was perhaps their names. - they will never see each other again, don't you think so?"

"Hum — I think so!" Miss Moon said.

"And don't you feel lonely sometimes? Have you had any parents, brothers, or sisters?" I asked her with a silly smile.

"Delft, I had too, oh well, all dreams and wishes are tended towards me. I'm pleased, beautiful, and so forth loved. I'm just far away from the earth. Remember, *'loin des yeux près du Coeur;* far from the eyes close to the heart. The more I try to forget, the more I fall in love." The Moon said.

"You say; *Goodbyes* are entirely for those who yearn with their minds because those who cherish with heart and soul there is no such thing as separation?"

"What separates admiration, gratitude, and platonic love?"

"Well, Delft, love are experiencing, and leaving behind."

I smirked, "Even if it's a pure passion?"

"Hey, do you want to die?" Then, Miss Moon strolled back into a piece of sky.

"I salute the God within you Miss Moon, I give you gratitude, I want to live my childhood again and mix my tears with the rain. You will give it back to me as a present, or do you just think it is thoughtless for you?"

"It is a secret, Delft; I will tell you the answer to that when we meet again."

"Miss Moon, I guess you do that. Guarantee me you will tell my parents that I will always love them. Persuade me that someday you will tell me the first wish that my mother made to you when she knew she give birth to me and saw my face. Assured me you will always listen to my wishes and pray for me." I said self-sacrificing.

"Good night, Delft," she said wistfully.

"Miss Moon, would you please tuck me in? And promise that, when we meet again, we will smile." I said selflessly.

"Use your talents to be a comfort to those who need it. Speak to your mountains or problems you have."

"Huh! Do you want to die? Only God can move a mountain."

"What? --" The Moon twinkled at me and slid under an opaque gray cloud,

> *"If the wind tickles your ears,*
> *it means that I am calling your name.*
> *When the wind is blowing, hold out your hand,*
> *the wind flutters past you, right?*
> *Know that I am holding tightly to your hand.*

Even if your eyes fill up, don't cry,
because I'll always be present by your side,
invisible, but only you can see me..."

Sad, happy, or tiresome memories, I love them all. They are a part of the water of my growth, the acknowledge my strength. Blinding teardrop-alike grief will come to pass away.

I was too tired. I closed my eyes as I lay down a load of my emotion, pain, and emptiness by my pillow, I slept ... a good night's sleep was valuable to redefine my strategies.

19 ~THE EYES OF PEOPLE

Exhausted after several weeks of applying and phone interview, I went to attend a workshop the event at the Peninsula Works one-stop, Daly City, California, a part of America's Job Centre network.

A man hearing my introduction said, "Delft how would you like to join my team of interns? You could teach many Job Seekers how to write a valid resume — it will make a world of a difference.

I wondered how this thing would have been different if — was I granted a chance at getting my social life back?

"Yes," I said.

I needed this volunteering assignment to sound as challenging as possible to my friends. The brochures for volunteering *at Peninsula Works your one-stop job connection, Daly City, California, said Peninsula Works internship was an opportunity to transform and affect positive change in the community. It was open to individuals of all backgrounds, college majors, and career interests.*

~ Chris B. Missett ~

The Peninsula Works The internship program was providing a learning environment and real-life career and personality development training.

Hal S. Kataoka, M.A. founded the internship program for the Human Services Agency in 1988 which since then has aided thousands of unemployed and their families in San Mateo County to learn job search strategies, increasing their skill sets and gaining the right attitude to be employable in the competitive job market. In many cases, in many people lives, there were many interests.

This meant that I had to give special attention to something that I loved to do.

The purpose of several personal goals have been to make progress and to show that I had become closer to impact someone else's life before I died — it could be a noble feeling!

I perhaps have been an orphan but, having life had been my mother's greatest gift.

The inner child in me had several goals I hoped to accomplish, but I have kept telling myself that I was one person — one person with limited education and resources.

I could only do so many things at one time.

Since the age of fourteen, I had enjoyed volunteering as a young Christian Catholic helping older people and helping low-income children.

I had always wanted to be different in another person's life. This feeling had always wavered in me as a precious gift from my mother.

I was so excited to get started. Through rewarding seminars and taught workshops, I found a new sensei master...teacher, in a Japanese samurai nephew Hal Kataoka.

I had never liked psychology, but the advanced clinical seminar of Myers Briggs and Kerseys Temperament had captivated me.

I discovered that I was introverted by the intuitive perception of feeling (INFP).

The INFP personality traits were open-minded, idealistic, flexible individuals and, dislike conflict.

To be honest, I didn't know if Hal influenced me to become an author by always calling me, "The Little Prince," a story written by a French pilot and author: Antoine de Saint Exupéry.

Over the course of the year, I devoted emphatically to the Interns team.

I was thankful for my personal growth, so satisfied with my experience and the set of creativities.

As a valuable representative of the Peninsula Works Internship team.

The San Mateo County, California, Human Services Agency awarded me with a commendation for the Senate's distinguished award from the State of California's Humanitarian Service, and received a certificate from the Trainee Team of 2010.

Until then, Hal, I will miss your advice. Once again, like a wreck, I had left a lifebuoy. Like a salmon, I swam against the current of the river of life.

I also received a Congressional Appreciation Letter from US, Congresswoman, Jackie Speier, for helping two job hunter training boot camps in 2010.

~ Weep, to a Beloved Destiny ~

Sayonara Sensei...

For the many seminars,
for helping me in your internship program,
for knowing how to interview
with confidence, and for having met you,
I had imprinted a huge impact in my life!

EPILOGUE

As I looked back at my life, it all begun with an act of imagination. At, fifteen and a half years old I did not love to walk away from home. I was not thrilled or satisfied with the journey.

Thoughts of the unconditional love from my mother were my gratitude and lingered in me. It was like a fable or a tale like the ones my mother used to tell us. I haunted by eyes, voices, and words of those I always left behind.

Each time, I was crossing a border of a new country; I was generating faith. It was the thrill of passing a new borderline, a venture of adventuring. My selfless often became a theater of isolation vs. fear failing.

On my journey, I played James Bond 007 and the characters of the children who survived the two world wars. I have never been so good. But my intuition and the dreams of my childhood were big.

I was combativeness with myself ... I was contesting with voices, forces, and ghosts that were whispering and telling me to continue to raise my own standards. Once in a while, I was alone for the first time in the ruthless reality of daydreams of a juvenile's original intentions.

My resilience and instinct became the essential elements to gain self-confidence. In the adventure, often, terrified by what could happen to me. The solitude was confusing.

The nostalgia of those I was leaving behind me was observing and witnessing me when no one in the living world knew or cared about.

I was challenging my thoughts; the victory was to conquer my own goals and fate. Everyone was once in my life is now a reflection. Everyone was filling the silence with their slow-witted or warm weight...

So forth, I had created a myth... My myth?

My Beloved Mom

God ties us to each other for eternity.
I want you to understand.
From, now even though we connect

by me holding your warmth of remembrances.

I am numb with the cold. Thrill and sadness
are just meaningless. You found me.
I have no basis for this,
but it absolutely is what I think.

Even though I slip away in the crowd,
we are looking up at the same sky.
Fragile, yet I want you to keep protecting me.
Let's meet up there again. I love you, Mom…

1

ABOUT THE AUTHOR

Chris B. Missett, son of MIA Vietnam Vet., was born in Ansbach, Germany in; raised in Germany and France.

Chris moved in The US, he self-financed his entire college education by working through school, educated in the US,

 He spends his spare time as a community service volunteer, cultivating his passion for IT, writing poetry, short stories, learning diverse cultures, and languages.

 Chris lives in Seattle, Washington, USA.

1
2

Made in the USA
Columbia, SC
01 January 2020